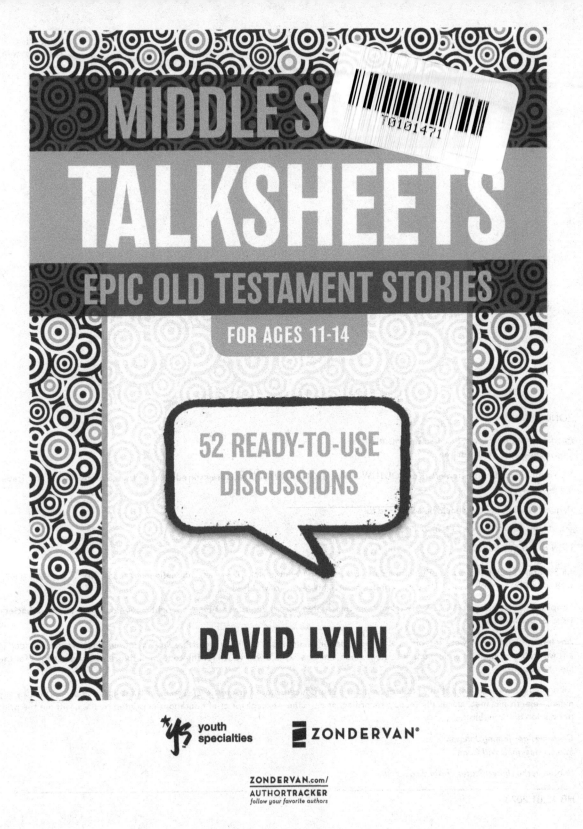

MIDDLE SCHOOL TALKSHEETS

EPIC OLD TESTAMENT STORIES

FOR AGES 11-14

52 READY-TO-USE DISCUSSIONS

DAVID LYNN

youth specialties

ZONDERVAN®

ZONDERVAN.com/
AUTHORTRACKER
follow your favorite authors

ZONDERVAN

Middle School TalkSheets, Epic Old Testament Stories
Copyright © 2012 by David Lynn

YS Youth Specialties is a trademark of YOUTHWORKS!, INCORPORATED and is registered with the United States Patent and Trademark Office.

Requests for information should be addressed to:

Zondervan, Grand Rapids, Michigan 49530

ISBN 978-0-310-88929-8

Cover design: Tammy Johnson
Interior design: David Conn

Printed in the United States of America

HB 12.01.2023

CONTENTS

THE HOWS AND WHATS OF OLD TESTAMENT TALKSHEETS

You are holding a very valuable book! No, it won't make you a genius or millionaire, but it does contain a year's worth of instant discussions to help middle school youth develop as disciples. Inside you'll find reproducible OLD TESTAMENT TalkSheets that cover 52 stories from creation to Gideon turning away from God—plus simple, step-by-step instructions on how to use them. All you need is this book, a few copies of the handouts, some young people (and maybe a snack or two), and you're on your way to landing on some serious issues in teenagers' lives.

These OLD TESTAMENT TalkSheets are user-friendly and very flexible. You can use them in a youth group meeting, a Sunday school class, or a Bible study group. You can adapt them for either large or small groups. And you can cover the material in as little as 20 minutes or explore it more intensively over two hours.

You can build an entire youth group meeting around a single OLD TESTAMENT TalkSheet, or you can use OLD TESTAMENT TalkSheets to supplement your other materials and resources. These TalkSheets are tools for you—but how you use them is up to you.

Middle School OLD TESTAMENT TalkSheets is not your average curriculum or workbook. This collection of discussions will get your young people involved and excited about talking through important issues. The OLD TESTAMENT TalkSheets deal with epic stories and include interesting activities, challenging talks, and thought-provoking questions. They'll get your youth forming new opinions, learning about themselves, and growing in their faith.

IMPORTANT GUIDING PRINCIPLES BEFORE USING OLD TESTAMENT TALKSHEETS

Let's begin by agreeing on two primary principles:

1. Faith is essentially caught not taught, and
2. The Holy Spirit alone works best to establish faith within teenagers' lives, changing them from knowers to believers, from church attendees to lifelong followers of Jesus.

If we can agree on these two principles, then it's easier to explain how OLD TESTAMENT TalkSheets is designed. It's not so much a teaching tool as a tool designed to engage real faith connections and encourage faith vocabulary in young people's lives.

So many church attendees don't know how to articulate their faith, nor do they often perceive vital connections to their faith outside the church building. Which is why OLD TESTAMENT TalkSheets' exercises are designed to help young people connect what they believe to their day-to-day lives, as well as develop a living faith vocabulary as opposed to a church vocabulary used only during church to please adults and religious leaders. For faith to grow with us throughout our lives, we must discover faith's vital connection in "real time." To see how and where Jesus in our lives engages the real world. And we must express this connection through a "vocabulary of faith" that grows with us and goes with us as opposed to expressing "church language" we reserve for religious settings and certain occasions.

Our Lord Jesus used the concept of fishing to connect his first followers with what he was doing, using words and images that were familiar to them. In the same way, you can use these OLD TESTAMENT TalkSheets to create settings in which young people can talk about faith, employing familiar concepts that help develop faith vocabulary and deepen faith by connecting it to relevant life experiences.

OLD TESTAMENT TalkSheets as an Engaging Tool More Than a Teaching Tool

I believe we've often made a very fundamental mistake in how we assist young people in developing their faith: We've hammered down on obvious answers to questions that they're often not even asking. And as a result youth can answer questions "correctly" but don't see why the answers are relevant to their daily lives.

Take for example the primary question of faith: *Who is your Lord and Savior?* The right answer, of course, is "Jesus Christ is my Lord and Savior." I've heard young people answer this question correctly for many years. But I've also witnessed many young people get stumped regarding what *Lord* means in a culture in which we're all our own sources of truth, or why we need to be saved when everyone is basically okay. We mistakenly believe that just having good information is enough. But the information needs vitality and relevance that youth can wrestle with.

This is why we believe that young people must understand the tensions of life from which questions arise and struggle with how to answer those questions before they hear how God addresses lordship and salvation in the person of Jesus Christ. Then we can ask, "If this is how life is, then who is YOUR Lord and Savior?"

By engaging young people inwardly—"INNER-gizing" them into a real dialogue about their lives, their perceptions, and their faith—we can create pathways upon which we can partner with them as they grow as disciples.

A Common Pitfall to Avoid

Faith development is often a multi-step process. Some things must be set in place before other things can be embraced. For example, we might say a person moves from A to B before moving on to C and eventually arriving at D; but many leaders mistakenly view the move from A to D as a simple task and grow impatient for those under their care to make that developmental leap. And people may be willing to make leaps they're not ready for because they trust their leaders or are afraid to express doubts in "unsafe" environments. They also may believe they lack faith and feel guilty. And sometimes people just want to fit in.

I've witnessed these conditions where real faith isn't deep enough to sustain the pressures of real life, and substitutional faith is worn like a garment in God's house. Such followers attend gatherings but cannot pray for themselves, hold a secret doubt and guilt, and often defer to leaders on all matters of faith. Jesus says such followers are like shallow soil on which the seed falls and eventually dies.

Instead good Christian leaders understand that they're guides on the roadside as people follow the master.

Essentially a discussion leader can fill three roles: A Tool, a Thorn, or a Stage Director:

Tool: A force in the hand of the Holy Spirit that works in a young person's life during the process of faith building.

Thorn: The leader becomes an irritant in disciples' lives, which can alienate them from the faith community due to the unsafe faith environment and unrealistic expectations and impatient discipleship methods.

Stage Director: Leader inoculates young people against "catching" real faith by creating an environment that encourages wearing masks of belief and speaking a kind of church language, effectively insulating them from embracing a real, vital faith expressed in a living language.

Clearly only one role serves well here: the Tool.

OLD TESTAMENT TalkSheets Can Help Us Be Good Stewards of a Sacred Process

But if we understand that deep, rich soil may take time and much mulching if a seed is to take root, then we can as leaders trust that faith is not about us achieving something in others' lives but about the Holy Spirit shaping followers' lives. We can become stewards of a most sacred process. Young people can pick up useless notions of faith and life on their way to discovering real faith through vital discipleship, and if these useless notions are to be replaced with life-giving awareness in a living, vital faith in Jesus, we must offer patience and loving mentoring.

Remember that Thomas didn't at first believe that Jesus was resurrected even though the other disciples expressed to him what they had witnessed. It's a great testimony of those early followers of Jesus that Thomas was still with them "in their midst" a week later when Jesus showed up and confirmed himself to Thomas. In the same way it's important to create a safe environment where youth can explore their faith and express themselves without the expectation of correct performance or the pressure to make a developmental leap that they're not ready to sustain as a disciple until, for them, Jesus shows up.

LEADING AN OLD TESTAMENT TALKSHEET DISCUSSION

OLD TESTAMENT TalkSheets can be used as a curriculum for your youth group, but they're designed as discussion springboards. They encourage your young people to take part and interact with each other while talking about real-life issues. And hopefully they'll do some serious thinking, discover new ideas for themselves, defend their points of view, and make decisions.

Youth today face a world of moral confusion. Teenagers are bombarded with the voices of society and the media—most of which drown out what they hear from the church. Youth leaders must teach the church's beliefs and values—and also help young people make right choices in a world full of options.

An OLD TESTAMENT TalkSheet discussion works to remedy this. While dealing with the questions and activities on the OLD TESTAMENT TalkSheet, your young people will think carefully about issues, compare their beliefs and values with others, and make their own choices. OLD TESTAMENT TalkSheets also will challenge your youth to explain and rework their ideas in a Christian atmosphere of acceptance, support, and growth.

One of the most common fears among middle school youth group leaders is, "What will I do if the young people in my group just sit there and don't say anything?" Well, when young people don't have anything to say, it's because they haven't had a chance or time to get their thoughts organized! Most young people haven't developed the ability to think on their feet. Since many are afraid they might sound stupid, they don't even attempt to figure out how to voice their ideas and opinions.

Again, OLD TESTAMENT TalkSheets let your youth deal with the issues in a challenging, non-threatening way before the actual discussion begins. They'll have time to organize their thoughts, write them down, and ease their fears about participating. They may even look forward to sharing their answers! Most importantly, they'll want to find out what others said and open up to talk through the topics.

If you're still a little leery about the success of a real discussion among your youth, that's okay! The only way to get them rolling is to get them started.

Your Role as the Leader

The best discussions don't happen by accident. They require careful preparation and a sensitive leader. Don't worry if you aren't experienced or don't have hours to prepare. OLD TESTAMENT Talk-Sheets are designed to help even the novice leader! The more OLD TESTAMENT TalkSheet discussions you lead, the easier it becomes. Keep the following tips in mind when using the OLD TESTAMENT TalkSheets as you get your young people talking.

Be Choosy
Each OLD TESTAMENT TalkSheet deals with a different story. Under the title of each OLD TESTAMENT TalkSheet is a subtitle expressing its theme; you can use the subtitle to choose an OLD TESTAMENT Talk-Sheet to match your group's needs and maturity level. Don't feel obligated to use the OLD TESTA-MENT TalkSheets in the order they appear in this book, either. Use your best judgment and mix them up however you want—they are tools for you!

Make Copies
Each student will need a copy of the TalkSheet—which is the right-facing page. The material on the reverse side (the Leader's Guide) is just for you. You can make copies for your group only—but *not* every group in your town!—because we've given you permission to do so. But U.S. copyright laws have not changed, and it's still mandatory to request permission from a publisher before making copies of other published material. Thank you for cooperating.

Try It Yourself
Once you've chosen an OLD TESTAMENT TalkSheet for your group, answer the questions and do the activities yourself. Imagine your young peoples' reactions to the OLD TESTAMENT TalkSheet. This will help you prepare for the discussion and understand what you're asking them to do. Plus you'll have some time to think of other appropriate questions, activities, and Bible verses.

Get Some Insight
On each Leader's Guide page you'll find numerous tips and ideas for getting the most out of your discussion. You may want to add some of your own thoughts or ideas in the margins.

Set Up for the Talk
Make sure the seating arrangement is inclusive and encourages a comfortable, safe atmosphere for discussion. Theater-style seating (in rows) isn't discussion-friendly; instead arrange the chairs in a circle or semicircle (or on the floor with pillows!).

Introduce the Topic
You may introduce the topic before you pass out the OLD TESTAMENT TalkSheets to your group and then allow the topic to develop as you use the material. We have a simple format on the Leader's Guide that can help your introduction: In the "Read Out Loud" section, simply read the paragraph/s aloud, then ask a young person to read the story from the Bible. After the story is read, you can use the question in the "Ask" section to get the group primed for a discussion of the story.

Depending on your group, keep your introduction short and to the point. Be careful not to over-introduce the topic, sound preachy, or resolve the issue before you've started. Your goal is to spark their interest and leave plenty of room for discussion, allowing the material to introduce the topic.

Now you're on your way! The following are excellent methods you can use to introduce any topic in this book—

- Show a related short film or video.
- Read a passage from a book or magazine that relates to the subject.
- Play a popular CD/DVD that deals with the topic.
- Perform a short skit or dramatic presentation.
- Play a simulation game or role-play, setting up the topic.

- Present current statistics, survey results, or read a newspaper article that provides recent information about the topic.
- Use an icebreaker or other crowd game, getting into the topic in a humorous way.
- Use posters, videos, or other visuals to help focus attention on the topic.

There are endless possibilities for an intro—you are limited only by your own creativity! Keep in mind that a clear, simple introduction is a very important part of each session.

Set Boundaries

It'll be helpful to set a few ground rules before the discussion. Keep the rules to a minimum, of course, but let youth know what's expected of them. The following are suggestions for some basic ground rules:

- **What's said in this room stays in this room.** Emphasize the importance of confidentiality. Some young people will open up easier than others, but if your youth can't keep the discussion in the room, then no one will open up.
- **No put-downs.** Mutual respect is important. If your young people disagree with some opinions, ask them to comment on the subject (not who made the comment). It's okay to attack the ideas, but not the people behind them.
- **There's no such thing as a dumb question.** Your group members must feel free to ask questions at any time. The best way to learn is to ask questions and get answers.
- **No one is forced to talk.** Let everyone know they have the right to pass or not answer any question.
- **Only one person speaks at a time.** This is a mutual respect issue, too. Everyone's opinion is worthwhile and deserves to be heard without competing voices.

Communicate with your group that everyone needs to respect these boundaries. If you sense that your group members are attacking each other or behaving otherwise negatively during the discussion, stop and deal with the problem before going on.

Allow Enough Time

Pass out copies of the OLD TESTAMENT TalkSheet to your young people after the introduction and make sure that each person has a pen or pencil and a Bible. There are usually five or six activities on each OLD TESTAMENT TalkSheet. If your time is limited, or if you're using only a part of the OLD TESTAMENT TalkSheet, tell the group to complete only the activities you'd like them to complete.

Decide ahead of time if you'd like them to work on the OLD TESTAMENT TalkSheets individually or in groups.

Let them know how much time they have to complete the OLD TESTAMENT TalkSheet and when there's a minute (or so) left. Start the discussion when everyone seems ready to go.

Set the Stage

Create a climate of acceptance. Most teenagers are afraid to voice their opinions because they don't want to be laughed at or look stupid in front of their peers. They want to feel safe when it comes to sharing their feelings and beliefs. Communicate that they can share their thoughts and ideas—even if they may be different or unpopular. If they hear put-downs, criticism, laughter, or snide remarks (even if their statements are opposed to the Bible) directed at them, it'll hurt the discussion.

Always phrase your questions so that you're asking for an opinion, not an answer. For example, "What should Bill have done in that situation?" should be rephrased with the simple addition of three words: "What *do you think* Bill should have done in that situation?" That makes the question more of an opinion and, therefore, less threatening;

you're not after them for the "right" answer. Your young people will relax when they feel more comfortable and confident. Plus, they'll know you actually care about their opinions and feel appreciated!

Lead the Discussion

Discuss the OLD TESTAMENT TalkSheet with the group and encourage all your young people to participate. Communicate that it's important for them to respect each other's opinions and feelings! The more they contribute, the better the discussion will be.

If your youth group is big, you may divide it into smaller groups of six to 12. Each of these small groups should have a facilitator—either an adult leader or a mature teen leader—to keep the discussion going. Remind the facilitators to not dominate the discussion. In fact, instruct facilitators to redirect questions or responses to the group if they keep looking for leaders for answers. Once the smaller groups have completed their discussions, combine them into one large group and ask the different groups to share their ideas.

Hint: You don't have to divide the groups up with every OLD TESTAMENT TalkSheet. For some discussions, you may want to vary the group size or divide the meeting into groups of the same sex.

The discussion should target the questions and answers on the OLD TESTAMENT TalkSheet. Go through them one at a time and ask the young people to share their responses. Have them compare their answers and brainstorm new ones in addition to the ones they've written down. Encourage them to share their opinions and answers, but don't force responses from those who are quiet.

Affirm All Responses, Right or Wrong

Let your young people know that their comments and contributions are appreciated and important. This is especially true for those who rarely speak up—make a point of thanking them for joining in.

This will be an incentive for them to participate further in future sessions.

Remember, though, that affirmation doesn't mean approval. Affirm even those comments that seem wrong to you. You'll show that everyone has a right to express their ideas, no matter how controversial. If someone states an opinion that's off base, make a mental note of the comment. Then in your wrap-up, come back to the comment or present a different point of view in a positive way. But *don't* reprimand the person who voiced the comment.

Don't Be the Answer Authority

Some young people believe you, as a leader, have the correct answer to every question. They'll look to you for approval. If they start to focus on you for answers or approval that they're "correct," redirect them toward the group by saying something like, "Remember that you're talking to everyone, not just me."

Your goal as the facilitator is to keep the discussion alive and kicking. It's important that your young people think of you as a member of the group—on their level. The less authoritative you are, the more value your opinions will carry. If your young people view you as a peer, they will listen to your comments more openly. You have a tremendous responsibility to be, with sincerity, their trusted friend.

Listen to Each Person

God gave you one mouth and two ears. Good discussion leaders know how to listen. Encourage others to talk first—then express your opinions during your wrap-up.

Don't Force It

Encourage all your young people to talk, but don't require them to comment. Each member has the right to pass. If you don't believe the discussion is going well, move to the next question or restate the question to keep things going.

Don't Take Sides

Be extra careful not to take one side over another. Instead encourage both sides to think through and even talk through their positions—ask questions to get them going deeper. If everyone agrees on an issue, you can play devil's advocate with tough questions and stretch their thinking. Remain as neutral as possible.

Don't Let Anyone (Including You) Take Over

Nearly every youth group has one person who likes to talk and is perfectly willing to express an opinion on any subject, all the time. Try to encourage equal participation from all the young people.

Let Them Laugh!

Discussions can be fun! Most of the OLD TESTAMENT TalkSheets include questions that'll elicit laughter and get youth thinking, too.

Let Them Be Silent

Silence can be scary for discussion leaders! Some react by trying to fill the silence with a question or comment. The following suggestions may help you to handle silence more effectively:

- *Get comfortable with silence.* Wait for 30 seconds or so to respond. You may want to restate the question to give your young people a gentle nudge.
- *Talk about the silence with the group.* What does the silence mean? Do they really not have any comments? Maybe they're confused, embarrassed, or don't want to share.
- *If you acknowledge the silence, it may break the ice.* Answer the silence with questions or comments such as, "I know this is challenging to think about . . ." or "It's scary to be the first to talk."
- *Ask a different question that may be easier to handle.* Or at least one that will clarify the one already posed. But don't do this too quickly,

without giving them time to think the first one through.

Keep It Under Control

Monitor the discussion. Be aware if it's going in a certain direction or off track. This can happen quickly, especially if there's disagreement or things get heated. Mediate wisely and set the tone you want. If your group gets bored with an issue, get things back on track. Let the discussion unfold but be sensitive to who is/isn't getting involved.

If a young person brings up an interesting side issue, decide whether or not to pursue it. If discussion is going well and the issue is worth it, let them talk it through. But if things get way off track, you might say something like, "Let's come back to that subject later if we have time. Right now, let's finish our discussion on . . ."

Be Creative and Flexible

You don't have to follow the order of the questions on the OLD TESTAMENT TalkSheet. Follow your creative instinct. If you find other ways to use the OLD TESTAMENT TalkSheets, use them! Go ahead and add other questions or Bible references.

Don't feel pressured to spend time on every single activity, either. If you're short on time, skip some items. Stick with the questions that are the most interesting to the group.

Set Your Goals

OLD TESTAMENT TalkSheets are designed to move toward a goal, but you need to identify your goal in advance. What would you like your young people to learn? What truth should they discover? What's the goal of the session? If you don't know where you're going, it's doubtful you'll get there. As stated earlier, there's a theme for each of the OLD TESTAMENT TalkSheets. You'll find this theme in italics under each of the TalkSheet titles.

Be There for Your Young People

Some young people may want to talk more with you (you got 'em thinking!). Let them know that you can talk one-on-one with them afterward. Communicate that they can feel free to talk confidentially with you about anything. Let them know you're there for them with support and concern, even after the OLD TESTAMENT TalkSheet discussion has been completed.

Close the Discussion

OLD TESTAMENT TalkSheets work best with a strong concluding presentation. You can use "The Close" section at the end of each Leader's Guide for this. Present a challenge to the group by asking yourself, *What do I want my young people to remember most from this discussion?* There's your wrap-up!

Sometimes you won't even need a wrap-up. You may want to leave the issue hanging and discuss it during another meeting. That way your group can think more about the issue, and you can nail down the final ideas later.

A FINAL WORD TO THE WISE—THAT'S YOU!

Some of these OLD TESTAMENT TalkSheets deal with topics that may be sensitive or controversial for your young people. You're encouraging discussion and inviting them to express their opinions, and as a result parents or others in your church who don't see the importance of such discussions may criticize you. So use your best judgment. If you suspect that a particular OLD TESTAMENT TalkSheet will cause problems, you may want to skip it. Or you may want to tweak a particular OLD TESTAMENT TalkSheet and only cover some of the questions. Either way, the potential bad could outweigh the good—better safe than sorry. And to avoid any misunderstanding, you may want to give the parents or senior pastor (or the person to whom you're accountable) copies of the OLD TESTAMENT TalkSheet before you use it. Let them know the dis-

cussion you're planning and the goal you're hoping to accomplish. Challenge your young people to take their OLD TESTAMENT TalkSheet home to talk about it with their parents. *How would their parents, as young people, have answered the questions?* Your young people may find that their parents understand them better than they thought! Also, encourage them to think of other Bible verses or ways that the OLD TESTAMENT TalkSheet applies to their lives.

1. Genesis 1:1-26

Creation 101

God created an awesome world—
including you!

1. On which day of creation would you have most enjoyed being by God's side?

Day 1: God creates light.
Day 2: God creates the sky.
Day 3: God creates the land, the oceans, and plants.
Day 4: God creates the galaxies including our sun and moon.
Day 5: God creates fish and birds.
Day 6: God creates animals and people.
Day 7: God rests.

2. Which of the following are most difficult for you to believe?

❑ God made me to be his friend. (John 15:12-14)
❑ God made me to do good things. (Ephesians 2:10)
❑ God made me special. (Psalm 139:13-14)
❑ God made me to tell others of Christ's love. (Ephesians 3:19)
❑ God made me to love my enemies. (Matthew 5:44)

3. Circle the one thing in creation that most shows God's power to you:

Butterflies   Mountains   Kangaroos   Rainbows   Hurricanes

4. Answer one of the following questions:

Which animal do you think God had the most fun creating?
Why do you think God rested on the seventh day?
What, in creation, shouts out that God loves you?
How does God's creation show his power to you?

5. How does God want us to take care of his creation? Check the one thing you are willing to do:

❑ Pick up litter I see and throw it away.
❑ Turn the lights off in rooms after I leave them.
❑ Learn more about recycling.
❑ Plant trees so that greenhouse gases are reduced.
❑ Turn the water off while brushing my teeth.
❑ Figure out a way for my family to waste less.
❑ Purchase products made from recycled materials.
❑ Reuse grocery sacks when I go to the store so that less plastic is left in landfills.
❑ You think of one: _____.

1. CREATION 101—God created an awesome world—including you!

(Genesis 1:1-26)

READ OUT LOUD

In the beginning God . . . At the get-go God . . . Starting out God . . . Creation is all about God —a God who intentionally thought through his creation culminating in the making of people in his image. It is because God created that we must take care of the world. It is because God created that we have value and are special. It is because God created that we are worth saving through the cross. (Have a student read out loud Genesis 1:1-26 for the story—or have group members read it quietly to themselves.)

ASK

What is the most awesome idea you've ever had?

DISCUSS, BY THE NUMBERS

1. This exercise helps your group members look at the different days of creation. You may get all kinds of questions related to evolution and creation. You don't have to have all the answers. The point of the first two chapters of Genesis is to emphasize that God is the creator of all things. Take some time to discuss the uniqueness of each of your group members. Read Psalm 139:14 and talk about how each of your group members was "fearfully and wonderfully made."

> *I praise you because I am fearfully and wonderfully made; your works are wonderful, I know that full well. (Psalm 139:14)*

2. Use this exercise to look at who God created you to be. The attached verses can be read to spark a discussion of God's design for your group members.
   • God made me to be his friend. (Romans 3:24)
   • God made me to do good things. (Ephesians 2:10)
   • God made me special. (Psalm 139:13-14)
   • God made me to tell others of Christ's love. (Ephesians 3:19)
   • God made me to love my enemies. (Matthew 5:44)

3. This exercise can help start a discussion of God's awesome power in creation. We often try to put God in a box. But God is all-powerful. Read Isaiah 55:8-9 out loud. Talk about how even though we can't always understand God's ways we can know that he is all-powerful, able to speak the universe into existence.

> *"For my thoughts are not your thoughts,*
> *neither are your ways my ways,"*
> *declares the LORD.*
> *"As the heavens are higher than the earth,*
> *so are my ways higher than your ways*
> *and my thoughts than your thoughts.*
> *(Isaiah 55:8-9)*

4. See commentary in bold after each question:
   • Which animal do you think God had the most fun creating? **Fun question for your group to discuss.**
   • Why do you think God rested on the seventh day? **God modeled rest and renewal for us. God did not need this rest and renewal but knew that we did, so he gave us the example. Talk about the importance of physical rest but also the need for spiritual and emotional renewal.**
   • What, in creation, shouts out that God loves you? **While all of God's creation speaks of his love, ask your group members to pick one thing.**
   • How does God's creation show his power to you? **Is it the vastness of the universe? The number of stars? The orderliness? What?**

5. Since we are created special by God, we have a responsibility to take care of God's creation. Spend a few minutes to talk about that responsibility and what it means practically.

THE CLOSE

The story of creation is much more than a list of what was created by God and when. It is the story of the unique creation of people—created special by God to have a relationship with him. Consider this for a minute. The God who spoke trillions and trillions of stars into existence created you to be friends with him.

Adam and Eve

God places us right where we're supposed to be

1. God placed Adam and Eve together in a beautiful garden called Eden. God has you spending the majority of your day in school. In what kind of school has God placed you?

❑ Home school ❑ Private school ❑ Public school
❑ Charter school ❑ Alternative school
❑ Juvenile court school ❑ Other

2. Go back to item #1. Why do you think God has you in the school situation you find yourself?

3. God expected Adam and Eve to do certain things in the garden he created. What things does God expect you to do where he put you?

❑ To tell others about Jesus ❑ To stay out of the way ❑ To be obedient
❑ To have people like me ❑ To impress people ❑ To do my best
❑ To be invisible ❑ Other: _____

4. God gave Adam and Eve only one rule in the Garden of Eden: To say "no" to eating from the Tree of the Knowledge of Good and Evil. Check off the items on the list below that you know God wants you to say no to:

❑ Chores ❑ Homework ❑ Internet games ❑ Alcohol ❑ Lying ❑ Texting
❑ Church attendance ❑ Sports ❑ Gossip ❑ TV ❑ Drugs ❑ Music

5. Did you know that God made Adam from a pile of dirt and formed him in his image? Just like Adam, you are a special creation of God who has been saved from sin by Jesus. So, why do you think you are here? What can you do right now with your life that will bring glory to God?

6. What advice do you think Adam or Eve might give you today? (You may check more than one.)

❑ Don't eat apples.
❑ Remember to thank God for what he has done for you and where he has placed you.
❑ Take better care of God's creation. It is important to God and should be important to you.
❑ Watch out for snakes.
❑ God created marriage as a good thing. No matter what your parents have done with marriage, honor marriage as a blessing from God.
❑ Enjoy the outdoors. It's a gift from God.
❑ God created everything but sin. Remember that.
❑ God made you special—even when you don't feel so special.
❑ Eat your vegetables.
❑ We messed up paradise here but God has a paradise waiting for us.
❑ Marriage is God's idea. Messing it up is the couple's fault.
❑ When in a garden, watch out for poison ivy.

READ OUT LOUD

Chapter two of Genesis is a retelling of the creation story of chapter one, expanding on the creation of man in the Garden of Eden. God tells the reader that Adam and then Eve were placed in a specific place with a particular job to do. So too, God has uniquely created each of us and placed us in specific places for his glory. (Have a student read out loud Genesis 2:7-25—or have group members read it quietly to themselves.)

ASK

What do you like most about the church in which God has placed you?

DISCUSS, BY THE NUMBERS

1. Listen to your group's school stories, including their grumblings.

2. This exercise gives you and your group the opportunity to talk about why God placed them in the school situation in which they find themselves. Instead of grumbling about where they are, focus on how God can use your group members where they are! Point out that we grumble too much instead of asking God to use us where we find ourselves. Ask, "How can God use you in the school in which you find yourself?"

3. Use this exercise to talk about what God wants them to be doing, not for their careers, but now. Focus on the important role God has for them— loving him with all their being and loving their neighbor.

4. God has placed your group members right where he wants them; but, like Adam and Eve, God has asked them to say no to certain things. This exercise gets you started in a faith conversation about saying no to the temptations that your group members confront in their schools, sports teams, and other situations. Ask, "Do you think you have more temptations than other people your age?"

5. We are uniquely different than God's other creations. We are created in God's image. Sin broke that image so it is no longer perfect, but Christ's death and resurrection has covered our sin if we have chosen to accept Christ's forgiveness. We

were created for a specific purpose, but we must choose to work toward that purpose. And we can be confident because *"it is God who works in you to will and to act in order to fulfill his good purpose"* (Philippians 2:13). Use this Bible verse as you listen to the answers to the questions, *So, why do you think you are here? What can you do right now with your life that will bring glory to God?*

6. The following checked boxes are things we can learn and take away from today's story.

   ☑ Remember to thank God for what he has done for you and where he has placed you.

   ☑ Take better care of God's creation. It is important to God and should be important to you.

   ☑ God created marriage as a good thing. No matter what your parents have done with marriage, honor marriage as a blessing from God.

   ☑ Enjoy the outdoors. It's a gift from God.

   ☑ God created everything but sin. Remember that.

   ☑ God made you special—even when you don't feel so special.

   ☑ We messed up paradise here but God has a paradise waiting for us.

   ☑ Marriage is God's idea. Messing it up is the couple's fault.

THE CLOSE

God places each of us in circumstances and conditions so that his will in our lives and the lives of others can be worked out. Are you glad that God chose you for his purpose? Are you excited about what God has for your life? Are you ready to move forward with God to work out his purpose in your life?

Temptation + Free Will = ?

God lets us choose our own life direction

1. During a week, how often do you think you are tempted to sin?

2. Answer the following three questions with a check mark. You can check more than one box.

   How are you like Adam?
   - ❏ I blame other people when I get caught doing something wrong.
   - ❏ My friends can get me to do something I know is wrong.
   - ❏ I don't talk to God when I have done something wrong.

   How are you like Eve?
   - ❏ I have talked others into doing things that are wrong.
   - ❏ I forget to think about what God wants me to do.
   - ❏ Sometimes doing bad things is fun.

   How are you like the snake?
   - ❏ I sometimes don't care what God would want me to do.
   - ❏ I don't think God's word applies to me.
   - ❏ I can get people to do what I want.

3. Adam and Eve knew that they had disobeyed God and they felt bad. What happens when you know that you have disobeyed God? (You can choose more than one answer.)

   - ❏ I never disobey God.
   - ❏ I tell myself it won't happen again.
   - ❏ I put God out of my mind.
   - ❏ Other: _____.
   - ❏ My stomach hurts.
   - ❏ I worry that God won't like me.
   - ❏ I hope I don't get caught.
   - ❏ I get mad at myself.
   - ❏ I say I'm sorry.

4. Matt and Zack were only a year apart. People often mistook them for twins. They were often called the "tiny terrors" when they were little. Now they were in middle school and the messes they got into were even bigger. And when they got caught they would always point to each other and say, "He did it!"

   Why do you think we like to blame others for our mistakes—for our sins?

5. Place a T on the line if you believe the statement is **True** or an F on the line if you believe it is **False**.

   __ Being disobedient doesn't affect my relationship with God.
   __ Adults sin more than kids.
   __ God still loves me even when I sin.
   __ I don't have to ask God for forgiveness; God knows what I'm thinking.
   __ It's not a sin if I don't get caught.
   __ God will punish me when I sin.

6. The same Satan that tricked Adam and Eve will try to trick me, too.

   ❏ I agree   ❏ I don't know   ❏ Disagree

READ OUT LOUD

God gave the first humans a free will. Adam and Eve could choose good or evil. The choice was theirs to make. They weren't robots but people with the capacity to decide their destiny. Satan, disguised as a snake, deceives Eve by getting her to question what God said. He distorts the truth of what God said. Adam stands by silent. (Have a student read out loud "The Fall" from Genesis 3:1-24—or have group members read it quietly to themselves.)

ASK

Can you name an actor, sports figure, or other celebrity that makes really bad choices? Really good choices?

DISCUSS, BY THE NUMBERS

1. Get estimates from your group members and come up with an average number of times they are tempted by sin during a week. The average will be a big number. Say something like, "This average shows how broken our world is. We are confronted by evil all the time. Like Adam and Eve, temptation stares us in the face. And like Adam and Eve we were created by God with a free will to say "yes" or "no" to that temptation.

2. God has given us the opportunity to make the choices that will decide our own life direction. We can ask God to make us more like Jesus. We can be satisfied to remain comfortable in our decision to become a Christian but not grow in our relationship with Christ. We can reject Christ altogether and opt for a religious belief system like Islam, atheism, or a New Age movement. Use this exercise to look at the bad choices that we sometimes make. Then talk together about strategies for dealing with those bad choices—the hows for turning our lives around when we have blown it like Adam and Eve did.

3. This item gives you the opportunity to talk about conviction of sin—those times when we know we have blown it and don't feel good about what we thought, said, or did. Discuss confession of sin (see 1 John 1:9). This is also the opportunity to talk about today's relative ethic when people only feel that they have done wrong when they get caught. Ask, "Why is something wrong whether you get caught doing it or get away with it?"

4. Eve blamed the snake, Adam blamed Eve, and the snake . . . well, the snake probably smiled. In this true-to-life situation Matt and Zack blamed each other. They get busy blaming everyone else for their disobedience. Think about a time that you blamed someone else for

something you did. Share with two other people what happened and how that worked for you. See how your group members answered the question, "Why do you think we like to blame others for our mistakes—for our sins?" Start a faith conversation about taking responsibility for our free will.

5. See commentary in bold after each statement:
   - Being disobedient doesn't affect my relationship with God. **Our disobedience blocks our relationship with God. We need to confess and turn from our sins to make our relationship right with God. Those who follow Christ, who put their faith in him, are forgiven. Period. Confession is a way to keep our relationship with God growing.**
   - Adults sin more than kids. **Not at all. Sin is not specific to a certain age.**
   - God still loves me even when I sin. **Yes he does. That love prompted God to send Christ to die for those sins.**
   - I don't have to ask God for forgiveness, he knows what I'm thinking. **Yes, God knows what we are thinking but asking him for forgiveness when we talk with God helps us get our relationship straight with him.**
   - It's not a sin if I don't get caught. **Not getting caught doesn't erase the sinfulness of our behavior. God knows and that's who we are sinning against.**
   - God will punish me when I sin. **God disciplines Christians for their sin so that we will learn. God punishes those who won't accept Christ's forgiveness.**

6. Some believe there is no Satan. Others believe Satan is behind every bush. The Bible declares that he is alive and well. He is not, however, behind every bush. But he is out there along with other fallen angels who wish to destroy those who follow Christ. Read 1 Peter 5:8 as you talk about the devil and his role in deceiving us.

> *Be alert and of sober mind. Your enemy the devil prowls around like a roaring lion looking for someone to devour.*

THE CLOSE

Today's story explains how people were broken because of sin. We are still broken today—every one of us. God didn't create us as mindless cyborgs but people with free will who voluntarily choose our actions. We can choose to follow Christ or to follow ourselves. What will you choose?

Cain Kills Abel

Which kind of faith do you have?

1. **Eve was grateful to God for his faithfulness, including giving her Abel. What do you do to show God you are grateful for his grace?**

   ☐ What exactly is grace?
   ☐ I thank God when I pray.
   ☐ I go to my church's worship service.
   ☐ I'm not sure God has been faithful to me.
   ☐ I made a list of all the things God has done for me.
   ☐ I tell God that I'm messed up and need his help.
   ☐ Other: _____

2. **Cain gave some veggies to God as a present. He thought he was good enough for God the way he was. Abel sacrificed the life of one of his lambs as an offering because he knew he needed God's forgiveness for his sins. What do you think about your sins?**

   ☐ My sins aren't bad enough to need God's forgiveness.
   ☐ I need God's forgiveness for some of my sins.
   ☐ I desperately need God's forgiveness for my sins.

3. **God talked with Cain about his sin problem. How does God talk with you about your sin problem?**

   ☐ I don't have a sin problem
   ☐ The Holy Spirit works through my conscience
   ☐ Through R-rated movies
   ☐ When I silently listen in prayer
   ☐ Through sermons
   ☐ Through small group Bible study
   ☐ Other: _____

   ☐ God doesn't talk with me
   ☐ Through my parents
   ☐ When I read the Bible
   ☐ Through fortune cookies
   ☐ Through the police
   ☐ When I get on Facebook®

4. **Cain walked away from God's offer to get right with him. Why do you think some people walk away from God even though they know better? T=True F=False**

   ____ They enjoy sin more than their friendship with God.
   ____ They believe they're missing out on something.
   ____ They want to be like their friends who don't know Jesus Christ.
   ____ They are stupid.
   ____ They believe they can get back with God just before they die.
   ____ They never really knew God in the first place.
   ____ They are mad at God.

   Then the LORD said to Cain, "Why are you angry? Why is your face downcast? If you do what is right, will you not be accepted? But if you do not do what is right, sin is crouching at your door; it desires to have you, but you must rule over it." (Genesis 4:6-7)

5. **Cain took his brother out into the field where no one could see them. That's where he murdered Abel. Why do people act like they can go off somewhere and hide their sins from God?**

READ OUT LOUD

Cain and Abel both brought offerings to God. Perhaps Cain and Abel had sisters who did the same thing along with their parents Adam and Eve. It was that time in which the family of Adam and Eve came before God to seek his forgiveness and ask for mercy. (Have a student read out loud the story found in Genesis 4:1-12—or have group members read it quietly to themselves.)

ASK

When do you most like to get together with God?

DISCUSS, BY THE NUMBERS

1. Eve was grateful to God for his faithfulness, including giving her Abel. What do you do to show God you are grateful for his grace? See commentary in bold after each statement.

   - What exactly is grace? **This item gives you the chance to have a faith conversation about God's undeserved mercy toward us.**
   - I thank God when I pray. **Our prayers can include more than our requests.**
   - I go to my church's worship service. **Corporate worship is one way to express our gratitude.**
   - I'm not sure God has been faithful to me. **Sometimes young people are mad at God (which he can handle) and miss recognizing his faithfulness. It's okay to be mad at God. He is big enough to handle it.**
   - I made a list of all the things God has done for me. **A gratitude list is an awesome way to thank God.**
   - I tell God that I'm messed up and need his help. **God always honors our confession (1 John 1:9).**

2. Start a faith conversation on the need for repentance of sin—the response of Abel.

3. See commentary in bold after each statement:
   - I don't have a sin problem—**We all have a sin problem even if we committed only one sin. Any sin breaks our relationship with God and needs God's grace to cover it.**
   - God doesn't talk with me—**Use this as an opportunity to start a faith conversation on the ways God talks with us.**

- The Holy Spirit works through my conscience—**The Holy Spirit can prompt us to change through guilt.**
- Through my parents—**Parents and other authority figures can be used by God to guide us.**
- Through R-rated movies—**Often they lead to sin**.
- When I read the Bible—**God's word has much to say about how we can deal with our sin problem.**
- When I silently listen in prayer—**The spiritual discipline of silence isn't something adults or young people often pursue. (Good opportunity to talk about silence and listening to God.)**
- Through fortune cookies—**Not.**
- Through sermons—**Yes, God speaks through the words of our pastors.**
- Through the police—**God even uses the police to talk with us about our sin problem.**
- Through small group Bible study—**Another opportunity to see what the Bible has to say.**
- When I get on Facebook®—**Could happen.**

4. Read Genesis 4:6-7 out loud. Look at each of the statements and decide as a group which are true and which are false. Then talk about ways to stay close to God. The best way to avoid drifting away from God is to focus on staying close.

   Then the LORD said to Cain, "Why are you angry? Why is your face downcast? If you do what is right, will you not be accepted? But if you do not do what is right, sin is crouching at your door; it desires to have you, but you must rule over it." (Genesis 4:6-7)

5. Talk about why, when we sin, we act like God is not around to see what we are thinking, saying, or doing.

THE CLOSE

God is calling us, through today's story, into a deeper faith that lasts—the faith expressed by Abel in his sacrifice. God is calling us into a faith that recognizes our brokenness and turns our faith around. God is calling us into a faith that makes him Lord rather than us. Is this a faith that appeals to you? If so, today is the day to surrender your life to Jesus Christ.

Lamech Is Wrapped Up in Himself

Get wrapped up in Jesus instead!

1. What kind of guy was Lamech?

- ❑ He was a nice guy.
- ❑ He was arrogant.
- ❑ He wanted to please God.
- ❑ He was easy to get along with.
- ❑ He was a guy who prayed all the time.
- ❑ He was a loving husband.
- ❑ He thought he knew more than God.

2. Your reputation is the opinion that others have of you. Lamech would have had a reputation of being hotheaded. What kind of reputation do you want to have?

- ❑ One cool dude
- ❑ A follower of Jesus Christ
- ❑ Class clown
- ❑ Brainiac
- ❑ Druggie
- ❑ Other: _____

3. Lamech was really wrapped up in himself. He was impressed with who he was instead of who God is. How can you get more wrapped up in Jesus than yourself?

- ❑ Get on my knees more when I pray.
- ❑ Pat myself on the back every time I achieve something.
- ❑ Recognize that Jesus is the one who created me.
- ❑ Brag all the time about my abilities.
- ❑ Tell myself how important I am.
- ❑ Thank Jesus for my abilities.
- ❑ Give Jesus the glory for my achievements.
- ❑ Not think less of myself but think more of others.

4. Lamech didn't care about God's opinion. Only his opinion mattered. So he did whatever he wanted. He married two women. He murdered someone.

- ❑ I am like Lamech. I do what I want.
- ❑ Sometimes I do what I want. Sometimes I do what God wants.
- ❑ I am not like Lamech. I care about God's opinion. I want to do what God wants.

5. *She's looking at me, Ben thought! The cutest girl in seventh grade just checked me out. Ben ducked into the bathroom and looked in the mirror. Yep, hair looks good; no zits, at least for now; and my new shirt looks good. What's not to love?*

Why would you want to be like Ben? Why would you want to avoid being like this?

READ OUT LOUD

Lamech is the seventh generation from Adam and Eve through Cain. Numbers are very significant in the Hebrew culture. Seven is a biggie so we should pay attention to the importance of this story. Remember that Cain killed Abel so this story can tell us the character and worldview that was produced from Cain's lineage. (Have a student read out loud the story from Genesis 4:16-24—or have group members read it quietly to themselves.)

ASK

Which celebrity do you believe is most wrapped up in herself or himself?

DISCUSS, BY THE NUMBERS

1. Lamech was certainly not a nice guy. He was a man who made up his own rules. He took two wives. He boasts of his bloody deeds. He is an arrogant man who meets insults with violence.
   - He was a nice guy.
   - He was arrogant.
   - He wanted to please God.
   - He was easy to get along with.
   - He was a guy who prayed all the time.
   - He was a loving husband.
   - He thought he knew more than God.
2. Ask, "Are you more like or unlike Lamech?" Talk about the kind of reputation the middle school-age young people in your area think is cool. Then talk about the reputation God wants you and your group members to have. Ask, "Why does God want his followers to have a good reputation among the world?" Read Philippians 1:27 in response to this question.

   Whatever happens, conduct yourselves in a manner worthy of the gospel of Christ.
   (Philippians 1:27)

3. See commentary in bold after each statement:
   - Get on my knees more when I pray—**While the position we take while praying doesn't influence God listening or not listening to our prayers, a kneeling position can help keep us focused on God.**
   - Pat myself on the back every time I achieve something—**While we need to take pride in what we do, we can too easily get caught up in ourselves rather than thanking God for our abilities and intellect.**
   - Recognize that Jesus is the one who created me—**Recognizing that we are created by Jesus gives us a proper perspective on our true selves.**
   - Brag all the time about my abilities—**Nothing but trouble for us. We are setting ourselves up for a fall.** *"Pride goes before destruction, a haughty spirit before a fall."* **Proverbs 16:18**
   - Tell myself how important I am—**In God's eyes you are enormously important. In your own eyes, not so much.**
   - Thank Jesus for my abilities—**Yes!**
   - Give Jesus the glory for my achievements—**While we do work hard and should be proud of that hard work, it is Jesus who gave us the talent.**
   - Not think less of myself but think more of others—**This is the C.S. Lewis definition of** *humility*.
4. We need to ask ourselves, 1) Does God have an opinion about the topic that concerns us (lying, cheating, spreading rumors? 2) What is God's opinion? And 3) Do I really care about God's opinion? Lamech was so wrapped up in himself that he didn't care about God's opinion. How about your group members?
5. Discuss the two questions: "Why would you want to be like Ben?" and "Why would you want to avoid being like this?" Add a third question to the discussion: "How could you avoid being like Ben?"

THE CLOSE

Jesus asked a simple question, "What good is it for someone to gain the whole world, yet forfeit their soul?" (Mark 8:36.) Lamech was so "into" himself that he shut God out. Here was a man who wanted to gain the whole world. He got wrapped up in himself and forgot about his soul. In whom will you get wrapped up—yourself or Jesus?

1. Enoch was remembered for walking with God. For what will you be (not hope to be) remembered if you died today?

- ❏ My great accomplishments
- ❏ My faithfulness to Jesus Christ
- ❏ My medals and trophies
- ❏ My grades
- ❏ The records I have set
- ❏ My athletic ability
- ❏ My good looks
- ❏ My musical talent
- ❏ My great breath
- ❏ My funny jokes
- ❏ My friendliness
- ❏ My coolness

2. Circle the one phrase that you think best describes "walking with God."

Putting me first

Desiring to do what God wants

Watching religious programs on TV

Listening to my parents

Trying to figure out God's opinion

Only telling little white lies

Asking God to help me be more like Jesus

Praying every day for others

Doing good works in the name of Jesus

Being good enough to get into heaven

3. God doesn't care so much about what you do but about who you are.

❏ Yes   ❏ No   ❏ Not sure

4. How many people do you know who have a great relationship with Jesus?

❏ Fewer than 5 people   ❏ 5 to 9 people   ❏ More than 10 people

5. Relying on whom?

- Katie won the first place trophy, again. Was there ever any doubt? Is Katie relying on her own efforts or relying on Jesus?
- Paul studied hard for the math test but took a deep breath and said a quick prayer. Is Paul relying on his own efforts or relying on Jesus?
- Sammy's parents were fighting again. Maybe if he left they would stop. Is Sammy relying on his own efforts or relying on Jesus?
- A popular girl in her class asked Destiny for a homework answer. Maybe if she gave it to her they could be friends. Is Destiny relying on her own efforts or relying on Jesus?
- *Boys never notice me*, thought Kenzie. *Maybe if I dress like some of the other girls they will.* Is Kenzie relying on her own efforts or relying on Jesus?

READ OUT LOUD

Like Lamech, Enoch is also the seventh generation from Adam and Eve. He is a descendant of Seth who was born after Abel was murdered by Cain. Seth, like the murdered Abel, was a follower of God. And like Cain who passed along his self-reliance, Seth passed along his God-reliance. (Have a student read out loud the story from Genesis 5:1-4, 21-29—or have group members read it quietly to themselves.)

ASK

What do you usually choose to eat for breakfast?

DISCUSS, BY THE NUMBERS

1. There is nothing wrong with good looks or athletic ability, unless it interferes with our relationship with Jesus Christ. Talk about what one needs to do to be remembered, like Enoch, for walking with God.

2. Debate which of the phrases best describe "walking with God." Use this exercise to discuss what it must have been like to be Enoch—to have been so close to God that he was taken to heaven without dying first. All we know about Enoch is that he was born, he was a father, and he walked with God. He loved God more than anything else in his life. He devoted his life to his creator. God was so pleased with Enoch that he took him and didn't let him experience death!

3. This is a great faith conversation starter. God cares at least as much about who you are as what you do.

4. Use this exercise to talk about Enoch role models, people your group members can look to so that they can see firsthand what it means to walk with Jesus Christ. Ask, "How are these people like Enoch?"

5. Like Enoch, we each have a choice. Enoch grew up under the influence of Seth, a parent who passed on his faith to the next generations. Yet, each generation has a choice to accept or reject a relationship with God. The choice is ours. We can choose the path of our parents or we can choose a different path. We can choose to rely on ourselves or on Jesus. Talk about each of the five situations and what it would look like to choose to rely on Jesus Christ or to choose to rely on one's own efforts.

- Katie won the first place trophy, again. Was there ever any doubt? Is Katie relying on her own efforts or relying on God?
- Paul studied hard for the math test but took a deep breath and said a quick prayer. Is Paul relying on his own efforts or relying on God?
- Sammy's parents were fighting again. Maybe if he left they would stop. Is Sammy relying on his own efforts or relying on God?
- A popular girl in her class asked Destiny for a homework answer. Maybe if she gave it to her they could be friends. Is Destiny relying on her own efforts or relying on God?
- *Boys never notice me*, thought Kenzie. *Maybe if I dress like some of the other girls they will*. Is Kenzie relying on her own efforts or relying on God?

THE CLOSE

Enoch, like Lamech, was the seventh generation from Adam and Eve. Lamech came from Cain who exemplified how to live by depending upon ourselves. Enoch came from Seth who showed how to live one's life depending upon the Lord. *"Enoch walked faithfully with God; then he was no more, because God took him away."* (Genesis 5:24) Don't you wish Enoch would have written a book, *The Five Steps to Walking Faithfully with God?"* Well, God did give us the Bible. And that's enough. We can walk with Jesus Christ just as Enoch walked with God. How? It's simple but not easy: *"For we live by faith, not by sight."* (2 Corinthians 5:7)

Noah Builds a Big Boat for a Big Flood

What does God want you to build?

1. If you could ask Noah one question about the challenges he faced by trusting in God's plan for him what would it be?

2. What do you think? **A=AGREE D=DISAGREE**

   ___ God's boat-building project strengthened Noah's faith.

   ___ Noah doubted God while building the big boat.

   ___ Noah built the boat because he was afraid of God.

   ___ Noah's family went along with Noah because they had no choice.

   ___ Hearing Noah's story strengthens my faith.

3. **Circle one:** It was **(fair or unfair)** for God to destroy humankind through the flood.

4. How do you think people today are like the people living in Noah's day?

   ❏ Most people today are like the people living in Noah's day.
   ❏ Half of people today are like the people living in Noah's day.
   ❏ Hardly anyone today is like the people living in Noah's day.
   ❏ No one today is like the people living in Noah's day.

5. Circle the one answer that best indicates who you are most like in the Noah story.

   Noah's neighbors   Noah's family   Noah

6. God asked Noah to build a boat, something that seemed foolish at the time. Noah obeyed. Why was it a good thing for Noah to do all that God asked him to do? What is one good thing God has asked of you that you don't want to do? Why is it a good thing for you to do it?

READ OUT LOUD

A world filled with evil. Increased population leads to increased sin. God is sad because of the rotten condition of a sinful world. We are not talking about today but the time in which Noah lived. So God decides to destroy humankind except for Noah and his family.

Now atheists, agnostics, and skeptics see this as an angry, unmerciful God waiting to punish anyone who crosses him. Not so. Throughout the Old Testament we see a holy and thoughtful God who doesn't take the punishment that humankind deserves lightly. He is not capricious but merciful. He doesn't take lightly the taking of human life. (Have a student read out loud the story found in Genesis 6:5-22—or have group members read it quietly to themselves.)

ASK

What is one thing your parents or grandparents ask you to do that you don't like doing? What is one thing they ask you to do that you love doing?

DISCUSS, BY THE NUMBERS

1. Use this question to get your group members to talk about the challenges they face as they trust in God's plan for their lives.
2. See commentary in bold after each statement:
   - God's boat-building project strengthened Noah's faith. **Ask, "How do you think your faith can be strengthened by facing these challenges head on?"**
   - Noah doubted God while building the big boat. **We all doubt—it helps us ask the questions that strengthen our faith. Share your doubt with God. He's big enough to more than handle it.**
   - Noah built the boat because he was afraid of God. **Noah respected God and obeyed.**
   - Noah's family went along with Noah because they had no choice. **Family life was different in the time of Noah, but everyone has a choice.**
   - Hearing Noah's story strengthens my faith. **Good conversation starter on faith.**
3. This is a time your group members can ask questions and vent their frustrations about the unfairness of God's punishment. People were so depraved by their sin that a holy God could no longer extend grace but was forced by his justice and righteousness to bring this sinfulness to an end. God is not vengeful or hateful, but a loving God that allowed people's sin to go on for years before he acted. The flood was the act of a righteous and loving God. People living at the time of Noah deserved what they got. Fortunately we are covered by the blood of Jesus. While we deserve death for our sins, the work of Jesus is our righteousness. Our punishment has been paid in full by Jesus. Read 2 Peter 3:9 out loud—*"The Lord is not slow in keeping his promise, as some understand slowness. Instead he is patient with you, not wanting anyone to perish, but everyone to come to repentance."* God's punishment for sin will come again. Like in Noah's day, God has been patient, but the day is coming when God's holiness and justice will again require punishment of sin for those who have not turned to Christ.
4. Read Genesis 6:5-6 out loud. Then talk about your group's answers to the question, "How do you think people today are like the people living in Noah's day?"

   The LORD saw how great the wickedness of the human race had become on the earth, and that every inclination of the thoughts of the human heart was only evil all the time. The LORD regretted that he had made human beings on the earth, and his heart was deeply troubled. (Genesis 6:5-6)

5. Noah's faith, like Abraham after him, was credited to him as righteousness. His obedience was evidence of his faith. Noah's family members appeared to follow Noah's example of faith. Noah's neighbors did what they thought was right in their own eyes. Begin a faith conversation with your group members about whom they are most like.
6. Every time Noah (and we) did what God asked of him, his faith or trust in God was strengthened.

THE CLOSE

God had a plan for Noah if he was willing to obey. God has a plan for your life—things for you to build. Are you ready to obey?

Getting into the Boat

What is God's ministry for you?

1. Noah's ministry included building a big boat, loading animals aboard that boat and taking care of those animals for up to a year while the world flooded. Would you have enjoyed this ministry if God had given it to you?

   ❑ No way. Have you seen that mess?
   ❑ I suppose but only if I have help cleaning up after the elephants.
   ❑ Well okay, I suppose I don't mind doing it.
   ❑ Sure. What a fun challenge.

2. Circle the five words that best describe what Noah was feeling as he loaded everything into the boat.

hurt	relief	grateful	confused	depression	disappointment
anger	acceptance	hopeful	fear	shock	helpless
guilt	sadness	resentful	numbness	emptiness	frustration
regret	anxious	overwhelmed			

3. A ministry is any activity done in the name of Jesus.

   ❑ I agree   ❑ I disagree   ❑ I don't know

4. Name an adult in your church who really enjoys serving Jesus Christ. How does ministry make this person's life exciting?

5. What can we learn from Noah's ministry? You can check more than one.

   ❑ Never give up.
   ❑ You might get a little wet doing ministry.
   ❑ Your family is part of your ministry.
   ❑ Ministry is exciting.
   ❑ Ministry can be hard work.
   ❑ Ministry is anything you do that serves God.
   ❑ Other: _____

6. When the alarm rang, Jessica rolled over and smacked the snooze button. Then she rolled back over for 15 more minutes of sleep. Suddenly she remembered it was her Sunday to help the worship band set up. The keyboard player promised to teach her how to play chords if she volunteered to help the band. Ugh. That sounded a lot better last Sunday afternoon than it did now at the crack of dawn. What was she thinking?

   How could Jessica help her congregation and God's kingdom through her ministry with the worship band?

READ OUT LOUD

To preserve Noah and his family plus the animals, God asked him to take on a big construction project—a nearly 500-foot boat. Can you imagine people making fun of Noah and his family as they finished constructing their huge boat on dry land far from water? What might Noah's neighbors have said? What might they have done? How do you think Noah handled the ridicule? And then imagine getting into the boat a week before the flood began. Until the rain began, Noah's construction ministry looked silly. But Noah obeyed God and entered the boat he had built with his family's help. He weathered the storm safely in the boat, taking care of the animals while God exterminated the evil outside the boat. He cleaned and fed and cleaned and fed. (Have a student read out loud about Noah's ministry from Genesis 7:1-24—or have group members read about it quietly to themselves.)

ASK

What is a ministry?

DISCUSS, BY THE NUMBERS

1. This exercise can get you started talking about the importance of ministry opportunities. See how enjoyable Noah's ministry would have been to your group members.
2. This exercise can get your group talking about ministry fears they may be having as you challenge them to get more involved in your congregation. Ask your group members to share their feelings. Ask, "Would you have these same feelings if you were asked to get more involved in the ministries of our church?"
3. Read 1 Corinthians 12:5-7 from the Contemporary English Version of the Bible found below as a good explanation of ministry. The statement "A ministry is any activity done in the name of Jesus" is a good definition of ministry.

> *There are different ways to serve the same Lord, and we can each do different things. Yet the same God works in all of us and helps us in everything we do. The Spirit has given each of us a special way of serving others.*
> *(1 Corinthians 12:5-7 CEV)*

4. Get some names of adults who serve. Your name will be mentioned. Tell stories of how ministry makes your life exciting and gives your life purpose and meaning.
5. Create a master list of all the boxes your group members checked about what they can learn from Noah's ministry.
6. Listen to answers to the question, "How could Jessica help her congregation and God's kingdom through her ministry with the worship band?"

THE CLOSE

Noah's ministry, from boat construction to zoo keeper, saved humanity from extinction. God chose Noah for that ministry as he has chosen you for a ministry. Noah could have said no just as you can say no. But by saying no, God will find another way to get his kingdom purpose completed. Say yes to ministry and be part of God's kingdom plan.

Noah Waits

God wants us to trust him while we wait

1. What is the longest period of time you have remained in your home without going out? How about in a car or bus? In a plane? How do you think Noah and his family felt stuck in the boat for about a year (40 days and nights plus the time it took for the land to dry out)?

2. How would you answer these—Y (yes) or N (no)?

Do you believe Noah and his family, during their year or so in the boat, learned to—

___ clean up after animals?
___ trust in God for their future?
___ talk to God every day?
___ exercise an elephant?
___ enjoy funny animal smells?
___ brush hay out of their hair?
___ be more patient with each other?

3. God didn't forget Noah, his family, or the animals waiting in the big boat. How do you know God hasn't forgotten you?

❑ The Bible says he hasn't forgotten.
❑ My family tells stories of God's faithfulness.
❑ I hear stories of God's faithfulness from members of my congregation.
❑ I've watched God in the past remember me.
❑ I think God has forgotten me.

But God remembered Noah and all the wild animals and the livestock that were with him in the ark, and he sent a wind over the earth, and the waters receded. (Genesis 8:1)

4. Noah and his family most likely talked often about God and their faith while they waited on the boat for the flood to end and the water to dry up. Who do you talk with most about God and your faith?

❑ Parents   ❑ Family members other than parents   ❑ Pastor   ❑ Other youth at church
❑ Other adults at church   ❑ Friends outside church   ❑ Other: _____

5. Josh's mom hasn't been feeling well for the last few weeks. She gets really tired and has a headache. And her symptoms have been getting progressively worse. Josh has been praying every night that she will feel better. It scares him to think that something could be really wrong with her. She has a doctor's appointment tomorrow to find out what's wrong. She told him that they will just have to trust God. This sounded easy when he was a little kid. Now with something this big, it is a lot harder not to worry.

What do you think Josh should do to worry less and trust God more?

READ OUT LOUD

Imagine being in Noah's sandals! You're on the boat you built with your family and animals—all kinds of animals. A storm is raging outside. You wonder if your boat-building skills were good enough. You try to relax. And now you wait. And wait. And wait to see what God does. (Have a student read out loud Genesis 8:1-16—or have group members read it quietly to themselves.)

ASK

Which of your pets do you trust the most to understand you when you are sad?

DISCUSS, BY THE NUMBERS

1. Use these questions to get your group to realize the amount of waiting they do in life. Say something like, "Whether we choose to put our faith or trust in Christ while we wait or act impatiently and grumble, we, like everyone else spend lots of time waiting."

2. Use this exercise to talk about the following. And yes, you can joke around about cleaning up after the animals and the funny animal smells.
   • trust in God for their future?
   • talk to God every day?
   • be more patient with each other?

3. Read Genesis 8:1 out loud. All of the statements are possible answers so take this opportunity to discuss each one.
   • The Bible says he hasn't forgotten.
   • My family tells stories of God's faithfulness.
   • I hear stories of God's faithfulness from members of my congregation.
   • I've watched God remember me in the past.
   • I think God has forgotten me.

   But God remembered Noah and all the wild animals and the livestock that were with him in the ark, and he sent a wind over the earth, and the waters receded. (Genesis 8:1)

4. Use this exercise as an opportunity to talk about the importance of daily faith conversations in everyday life. Discuss how your group members can increase the amount of faith conversations in their daily lives—with family, friends, and church members. The benefits—encouragement, increase in biblical knowledge, and spiritual growth.

5. Use this true-to-life situation to start a faith conversation around the question, "What do you think Josh should do to worry less and trust God more?" Tell a story of how God has helped you worry less and trust God more. Read Philippians 4:6-7 out loud to talk about a strategy for Josh and your group members.

   Do not be anxious about anything, but in every situation, by prayer and petition, with thanksgiving, present your requests to God. And the peace of God, which transcends all understanding, will guard your hearts and your minds in Christ Jesus. (Philippians 4:6-7)

THE CLOSE

God often asks us to wait. When we pray there are three answers God gives us—yes, no, or wait. Waiting on God is often difficult. We are, after all, humans who want what we want and we want it now. But God knows it is in the waiting that we learn to trust in him. It is in the waiting that we can grow closer to Jesus. It is in the waiting that we learn to be patient. It is in the waiting that we find the joy of following a God who can be trusted. So let's get going and learn to wait.

The Rainbow Promise

A reminder of God's faithfulness to us

1. God blessed Noah and his family once they were off the boat. How has God blessed you?

- ❏ God could care less about me.
- ❏ God encourages me with his presence in my life.
- ❏ God helps me work through my problems.
- ❏ God forgives me of my sins.
- ❏ God takes care of my needs.
- ❏ God is my friend when others abandon me.
- ❏ God cries with me and laughs with me.

2. Since the rainbow is God's promise to us, what should we do when we see a rainbow?

- ❏ Ignore it
- ❏ Remember God's promises
- ❏ Worship it
- ❏ Pray
- ❏ Dream about sailing or surfing
- ❏ Thank God for his faithfulness
- ❏ Other: _____

3. God didn't mess around with the evil in the world at the time of Noah. He destroyed everyone, except for eight people—Noah and his family. Noah had put his faith in God. Why do you think God would wipe out so many people? T=True F=False

- ___ God was having a bad day.
- ___ God takes sin seriously because God is holy.
- ___ The evil plans and actions of people were too much for God to tolerate.
- ___ The people laughed at Noah.
- ___ The people deserved it.
- ___ God enjoys violence.

4. God is a God who likes to show mercy. He promised Noah, and us, never to destroy the world even though it is filled with evil through a flood again. Jonah also learned this lesson. Read Jonah 4:2 found below. Then circle the one characteristic of God that you need the most right now.

I knew that you are a gracious and compassionate God, slow to anger and abounding in love, a God who relents from sending calamity. (Jonah 4:2b)

Gracious and compassionate—God gives chance after chance after chance.
Slow to anger—God is unbelievably patient and doesn't lose his temper.
Abounding in love—God loves like you've never experienced before.
A God who relents from sending calamity—God doesn't want to punish.

5. The Bible is filled with the promises of God. Connect the Bible verse on the left with the promise on the right.

1 John 2:25	Rescue from Fear
James 1:5	End of Suffering
John 14:2-3	Personal Peace
Revelation 21:4	Wisdom
1 John 1:9	Eternal Life
Psalm 34:4	Forgiveness of Sins
Isaiah 26:3	Christ Coming Again

READ OUT LOUD

The world is humbled to one family—Noah's. It is with this one family that God makes an agreement called a covenant in the Bible that he no longer wants to destroy the world through a flood. Instead he wishes a covenant friendship with those who choose it. God placed the rainbow in the sky as a symbol of his desire to be our friend—a sign of his covenant (an agreement) promise with us. (Have a student read out loud the story found in Genesis 9:1-17—or have group members read it quietly to themselves.)

ASK

What do you hate most about broken promises?

DISCUSS, BY THE NUMBERS

1. Encourage a faith conversation on the blessings we get with our relationship with God. Like the blessing given to Noah and his family, God blesses those who are faithful to him with all kinds of spiritual blessings.
2. Rainbows can be a great reminder of God's faithfulness to followers of Christ. While we don't need to worship rainbows we can remember that it is a symbol of God's desire to be friends with us (God's covenant relationship).
3. God has always taken sin seriously because he is holy. The people living in the time of Noah deserved death because of their evil ways—their evil plans and actions were too much for God to tolerate. Thank God for Jesus, who has covered our sin with his sacrifice. Today the word *sin* is rarely used in our secular culture. The impact of sin on daily living is minimized. Repentance is discounted as weakness. Ask, "What are the consequences of seeing sin as no big deal?"
4. Read Jonah 4:2b out loud. Ask volunteer group members to share the one characteristic of God that they need right now and why.

> *I knew that you are a gracious and compassionate God, slow to anger and abounding in love, a God who relents from sending calamity.*
> *(Jonah 4:2b)*

5. If time permits talk together through each of the promises of God. Discuss his faithfulness to Noah and to us versus our lack of faithfulness to him. See the correct connections below:

1 John 2:25	Eternal Life
James 1:5	Wisdom
John 14:2-3	Christ Coming Again
Revelation 21:4	End of Suffering
1 John 1:9	Forgiveness of Sins
Psalm 34:4	Rescue from Fear
Isaiah 26:3	Personal Peace

THE CLOSE

Rainbows are a reminder to us of God's faithfulness. We often forget that he wants to be our friend. The rainbow is a symbol of that friendship promise never to destroy the world again through floodwaters.

The Tower of Babel

What happens when we believe we know—better than God—what's best for us?

1. **Adults know what is best for young people.**

   ❑ I strongly agree ❑ I agree
   ❑ I disagree ❑ I strongly disagree

2. **The tower builders motivated each other to move forward with their plan to build a city with a tower—something God wanted them *not* to do. How do you encourage others to do good rather than evil?**

   ❑ Pray for my friends
   ❑ Respect my parents
   ❑ Refuse to spread rumors
   ❑ Make peace
   ❑ Say something when a friend puts someone else down
   ❑ Participate in church to learn more about God's way of doing things
   ❑ Invite my friends to church
   ❑ Do my best in school
   ❑ Watch my language
   ❑ Do something when I see bullying
   ❑ Talk to a trustworthy adult when I'm not sure what to do
   ❑ Other: _____

3. **The builders of the tower wanted to get to heaven their way. How do people your age think they will get to heaven?**

   ❑ Do more good than bad. ❑ Go to church. ❑ They don't believe in heaven.
   ❑ Pray often. ❑ They don't really think about Jesus or heaven.

4. **"That's it," said Simone. She just thought of a perfect project for her school's science fair. She had been searching for a topic for weeks. It needed to be the best so that she could beat David who won the science fair for the last two years. *That won't happen again*, thought Simone. This year she would be the winner.**

   The tower builders' wanted power and popularity. How is Simone like the tower builders? Are you more like or unlike the tower builders?

5. **Why do you think the tower builders were so intent on disobeying God? Check your top two.**

   ❑ It was no fun to do what God wanted.
   ❑ They were mad at God.
   ❑ They didn't care about God's opinion.
   ❑ They wanted to be like God.
   ❑ It was easier to do what they wanted.
   ❑ They never thought about what God wanted.
   ❑ They thought their way was best.

READ OUT LOUD

God had commanded Noah and his family to "...*be fruitful and increase in number and fill the earth*" (Genesis 9:1). But in today's story we see that the people defied God's wishes. Instead, they wanted to do what they wanted to do. It was all about "my" plan rather than God's plan. So God frustrated their mission so that his purposes would be accomplished. If God would not have intervened then the people would not have populated the earth. Instead they would have congregated their evil ways into one place, ultimately destroying themselves. (Have a student read out loud the story found in Genesis 10:32-11:9—or have group members read it quietly to themselves.)

ASK

When was the last time you had to ask for help?

DISCUSS, BY THE NUMBERS

1. "Adults know what is best for young people." This is a controversial statement that can make for a lively discussion. The point of the discussion is to focus on the fact that most people will argue for adults or for young people. For most people, God never enters the equation.

2. Read Genesis 11:4 below. The tower builders were doing evil because they were building for their own glory rather than for God's. They were commanded by God after the flood to scatter, not gather together. Yet, here they were congregated together doing their own will rather than God's. Talk about how evil behavior is always about self-glorification while good behavior gives glory to God.

> Then they said, "Come, let us build ourselves a
> city, with a tower that reaches to the heavens,
> so that we may make a name for ourselves;
> otherwise we will be scattered over the face of
> the whole earth." (Genesis 11:4)

3. Building the tower was a slap upon God's face—an insult that said, "God, we can get to you our way!" Talk about how people today are like the tower builders, desiring to be close to God on their own terms without having to be holy, to confess their sins and accept the forgiveness that Christ's death and resurrection offers them. See commentary in bold after each statement:
   - Do more good than bad. **This is a popular belief even for some Christians. This is contrary to the** gospel that says it is by God's grace through Christ that we are saved rather than our own good works.
   - Go to church. **We don't get any points or extra credit for church attendance. We do get to grow together in Christ but it isn't our church participation that saves us.**
   - They don't believe in heaven. **Refusing to believe in heaven or hell doesn't make either of them go away.**
   - Pray often. **Yes, prayer is a good thing—a spiritual discipline we practice to get closer to God after we are saved. Praying doesn't get us into heaven.**
   - They don't really think about Jesus or heaven. **Putting Jesus out of one's mind doesn't negate the reality of sin and the need for forgiveness.**

4. How is Simone like the tower builders? Are you more like or unlike the tower builders?

   The tower builders were driven by pride, a desire for prestige and power, and self-centeredness. Together answer these questions, focusing on Simone's motives as well as our motives for wanting to achieve anything.

   Do we wish to honor ourselves or God?

5. God had commanded Noah and his family to "...*be fruitful and increase in number and fill the earth*" Genesis 9:1. Yet, the tower builders actively schemed to go against God's command. Instead they wanted to do things their way. God confused the languages of the tower builders so that his will would be done. Talk together about the consequences of our thinking that we know what's better for us than God. Discuss each of the choices:

   It was no fun to do what God wanted.
   They were mad at God.
   They didn't care about God's opinion.
   They wanted to be like God.
   It was easier to do what they wanted.
   They never thought about what God wanted.
   They thought their way was better.

THE CLOSE

God wanted the tower builders to scatter throughout the earth. They thought they knew better than God so they congregated together and built their feeble tower in an attempt to reach God on their own terms. What happens when we think we know what's better for us than God does? Disaster every time! Let's trust that the Lord knows what is best for us and follow his ways.

1. Abram obeyed the Lord and moved to a new land. How easy is it for you to obey Christ?

- ❑ It's easy all the time.
- ❑ It's easy most of the time.
- ❑ It's easy some of the time.
- ❑ It's never easy.

2. Abram chose to follow God. Decide if the following situation is an example of following Christ or following your selfish desires.

	Following Christ	Following My Selfish Desires
a. Dressing in the latest styles	❑	❑
b. Thinking of others more than yourself	❑	❑
c. Spreading a rumor to hurt someone who hurt you	❑	❑
d. Studying for a math test	❑	❑
e. Texting a friend who is sad	❑	❑
f. Sleeping in Sunday morning after a late Saturday night youth event	❑	❑
g. Talking only to my Christian friends	❑	❑

3. Isabel promised God that she wouldn't swear anymore. It was well known that Isabel had a "potty mouth." Sometimes she just couldn't help it and sometimes she did it just to shock people. It would be hard not to swear but she was willing to do it if it meant that God would answer her prayer for a passing grade in her social studies class. Right now that didn't look like it was going to happen. It was Mr. Anthony's fault. He just didn't like her. So now it was up to God. She would be obedient, but she just better get that passing grade.

Abram obeyed God and God blessed him. Is Isabel being obedient to God by stopping her swearing? Should God manipulate Mr. Anthony into giving her a passing grade? Does obedience to God pay off?

4. Abram moved to the land of Canaan. He had to live with the Canaanites who worshiped false gods and would have tempted him with evil. Do you think you have it easier or more difficult than Abram with the kinds of temptations you face?

- ❑ I have it much more difficult than Abram.
- ❑ I have it about the same as Abram.
- ❑ I have it much easier than Abram.

5. God was present with Abram every step he took. I know for certain that God is with me every day.

❑ YES   ❑ NO   ❑ MAYBE SO

6. Are you ready to do something new and exciting for God? What?

- ❑ Prepare to be a missionary in a Muslim nation.
- ❑ Go to a third-world country on a mission trip.
- ❑ Write letters of encouragement to Christians.
- ❑ Play in a Christian band.
- ❑ Volunteer at a soup kitchen.
- ❑ Invite a kid to your church who is a loner.
- ❑ Join a Christian club at school.

READ OUT LOUD

Abram was asked by God to move to a country he had never seen. He could have refused. But by faith he picked up and moved forward. God blessed him for his obedience. (Have a student read out loud the story found in Genesis 12:1-8—or have group members read it quietly to themselves.)

ASK

What would be the hardest part for you if you had to move tomorrow to another country?

DISCUSS, BY THE NUMBERS

1. Use this activity to get a faith conversation going regarding the struggles group members face in following Jesus. Sometimes it's easy while other times it's quite difficult. Discuss both—what makes it easy and what makes it difficult?

2. Forward movement with God is all about following his ways rather than our own. God may not want your group members to move to a new country but he is calling them to move forward in their relationship with Jesus Christ. Use this activity to help your group members learn to discern the difference between following Christ and following selfish desires.

3. Making deals with God is not how we win his favor. Isabel had it all wrong. God wants us to be obedient. God blessed Abram for his obedience in moving. God continues to pour out blessings for our obedience. Blessing sometimes comes in the form of avoiding negative consequences of sin. Other times a blessing comes with the miracle of healing or financial blessing. And God blesses us even when we are not faithful. But bargaining with God when she hadn't done her part is not going to work with God. We can't manipulate God. He is a much bigger God than that.

4. Start a faith conversation about the temptations your group members face. Make a quick list of the top ten temptations. See if there is consensus among your group members regarding who has (or had) it more difficult—Abram or your group. Ask why.

5. Use this item to have a faith conversation regarding the importance of worshiping God—experiencing his presence in our lives. Discuss why corporate worship or worship with your congregation is also important in experiencing God's presence.

6. Here is your opportunity to challenge your group members (like God challenged Abram) to move forward and do something new and exciting with God. Ask, "What could you do together as a group that would be new and exciting with God?" "What could you as individuals commit to do by yourself or with your families?"

THE CLOSE

God called Abram to a new place and a new ministry. God is also calling you to a new place and a new ministry. God refuses to leave you where you are. He wants you to grow in your relationship with him. Today is your opportunity to commit to move forward to an exciting life with Jesus that will never be dull or boring. Christ has the power to make your life exciting and purpose-filled.

1. Andy looked at his new phone. It could do everything! He could even see the person he was talking to. His science teacher talked about how far things had come since he was in college. They didn't even have cell phones then. That was like the dark ages! In church the pastor was talking about how powerful God was in the Old Testament. That was probably because they didn't have stuff like we do now.

Abraham Believes the Lord

What do you believe?

How powerful do you think God is today?

2. God did the impossible in Abraham's life—he gave him a son. What do you think?

Answer **Yeah (I agree), Nah (I disagree),** or **Duh (I don't know).**
_____ God doesn't perform miracles today.
_____ God only does the impossible for really good people.
_____ I have seen God do impossible things in the lives of others.
_____ God is not as powerful today as he was in the Old Testament time of Abraham.
_____ I wish God would surprise me with a miracle in my life.

3. Circle the three words that best describe what you feel while waiting for the Lord to answer your prayers.

Anxious	Excited	Discouraged	Frustrated	Impatient	Faithful
Hopeful	Happy	Peaceful	Silly	Uncomfortable	Scared

4. Abraham believed God's promise for a son even though he and his wife Sarah were very old. This is how Abraham got into heaven; not by doing anything himself but by putting his faith in the Lord. If you trust in Jesus for the forgiveness of your sins then God credits that to you as righteousness. How often do you doubt your salvation?

❑ All of the time
❑ Some of the time
❑ Hardy ever
❑ Never

Abram [Abraham] believed the LORD and he credited it to him as righteousness. (Genesis 15:6)

5. Abraham has a covenant or friendship relationship with God. How is your relationship with Jesus?

❑ Who is Jesus?
❑ It's gotten worse over time.
❑ It's about the same as it has always been.
❑ It's getting better and better.
❑ BFFs—It's the best.

13. ABRAHAM BELIEVES THE LORD—What do you believe?

(Genesis 15:1-21)

READ OUT LOUD

You may remember that God made a covenant (an agreement) with Noah. God placed the rainbow in the sky as a symbol of his desire to be our friend—a sign of his covenant promise with us. God continues the covenant friendship with Abraham. God credits Abraham's faith in him as righteousness. God accepted Abraham as a righteous or holy person, no longer separated from God because of his sins. (Have a student read out loud the story found in Genesis 15:1-21—or have group members read it quietly to themselves.)

ASK

What do you believe is the best thing to eat for breakfast?

DISCUSS, BY THE NUMBERS

1. God demonstrated his power in awesome ways in the Old Testament. But often people see God as somehow less powerful today. God is the same God today as he was in the Old Testament. God can and does act powerfully today. Ask, "Are we looking at the ways God acts in today's world?" "Does our stuff distract us from looking to God today?"

2. Use this activity to talk about the impossible things God does every day. Tell a story of an impossible situation in your life in which God worked. See commentary in bold after each statement:

   • God doesn't perform miracles today. **God is in the miracles business. He performs them around the world every second. Keeping the universe from falling apart is a miracle.**

   • God only does the impossible for really good people. **God's common grace (means that we get rain during droughts and the sun rises every day) is given to everyone. Also nobody can ever be good enough to deserve God's grace.**

   • I have seen God do impossible things in the lives of others. **Tell a story of how you have seen this.**

   • God is not as powerful today as he was in the Old Testament time of Abraham. **God is the same today as he was in the Old Testament. Our stuff often distracts us from seeing God's power.**

   • I wish God would surprise me with a miracle in my life. **Identify the miracles that God is already performing. That's easy—create a gratitude list.**

3. We too often get impatient and take matters into our own hands rather than wait for God to act. This sin keeps us from experiencing all of God's goodness in our lives. Talk about how difficult it can be to wait upon the Lord as well as the benefits of being patient.

4. We do the same thing. We doubt. Discuss some of the other doubts your group members have had. Challenge your group members to examine their doubts, to ask questions and seek out answers from God.

5. Use this exercise to converse with your group about your and their relationship with Jesus. Explore why their relationship with Jesus is getting better, staying the same, or getting worse.

THE CLOSE

The question is a simple one, "What do you believe?" Yet, the answer has profound implications for eternity. Our belief in Jesus Christ sets us apart from other religions because Christianity is about a relationship rather than our efforts to reach God. What we believe is important. It guides the direction and purpose of our lives. In Christ we have a living hope in the present and for the future. What are you going to believe?

The Evil of Sodom and Gomorrah

You can avoid sinful circumstances—
it's your decision

1. The sinfulness in Sodom affected Lot and his family. How easy is it for you to resist or run from the sinfulness at your school, in your after-school activities, and on TV and the Internet?

- ❑ Really, really easy
- ❑ Somewhat easy
- ❑ Somewhat difficult
- ❑ Really, really difficult

2. Who helps you the most to avoid sin?

- ❑ My parents
- ❑ My best friend
- ❑ Church friends
- ❑ Facebook®
- ❑ Listening to God by reading my Bible
- ❑ Teachers and other adults at school
- ❑ Other: _____

3. The two men engaged to Lot's daughters chose to ignore the angels' warning. How do you think God warns you before you make bad choices?

- ❑ Gives you parents and other adults who care about your choices
- ❑ Develops your conscience so you can tell right from wrong
- ❑ Sends you text messages
- ❑ Offers spiritual and moral direction in the Bible
- ❑ Plants messages in fortune cookies
- ❑ Prompts you through the Holy Spirit that your choice is a bad one
- ❑ Uses Christian music to encourage you
- ❑ Other: _____

4. Destiny's parents were always saying, "If everyone jumped off a cliff would you do it too?" when they talked to her about peer pressure. She thought she was doing just fine handling the temptations that came her way. She could be with her friends in tempting situations and say "no" even when her friends said "yes." She didn't want to be thought of as a "goody-goody."

Do you think Destiny is doing okay at handling herself around temptation?

5. Lot and his two daughters had to be rescued from Sodom or else they would have been destroyed. Which of the following might destroy you?

- ❑ My desire to try alcohol or other drugs like marijuana
- ❑ My laziness in school
- ❑ My bad friendship choices
- ❑ My resistance to reading the Bible
- ❑ My lack of exercise
- ❑ My skipping church activities
- ❑ Other: _____

READ OUT LOUD

The wildly popular story of Sodom and Gomorrah is known more for its depravity than for Lot and his family. The angels of the Lord come to Sodom where Lot and his family live to rescue them from the coming destruction of both the cities of Sodom and Gomorrah. It is often assumed that God was a raging God of vengeance in the Old Testament and changed somehow to the God of love found in the New Testament. When we assume this we fail to see that God has always been the God of love, mercy, and patience. But God is also holy and can only stand evil for so long. His patience is up for the evil disaster that had become Sodom and Gomorrah. (Have a student read out loud the story of Lot's rescue found in Genesis 19:12-29—or have group members read it quietly to themselves.)

ASK

What's the worst natural disaster you've ever experienced—hurricane, earthquake, fire, tornado, flood?

DISCUSS, BY THE NUMBERS

1. Place the following on a whiteboard or flip chart paper.

   School—
   After- School Activities—
   TV—
   Internet—
   Other—

   Make a list of the temptations that pull your group members toward sin in each of the categories. Then use the rating system in this exercise to see how easy or difficult it is for your group members to resist or run from each listed area (school, after school, TV, Internet, other).

2. Begin a faith conversation about the importance of others in helping us to live for Jesus. Tell a story of how your Christian friends and relatives have helped you in the past avoid sin. Find out which of those on the list help your group members the most in avoiding sin. Ask, "Why were they such a big help?"

3. Use this exercise to talk practically about God's warning system. God gives us plenty of warnings through parents and grandparents, friends, preaching of the Word, the Bible, Christian music, and the prompting of our consciences by the Holy Spirit. Ask, "How have you acted like Lot's almost sons-in-law and ignored warnings?" Ask, "Have you been made fun of for trying to get a friend to do the right thing?"

4. Discuss the question, "Do you think Destiny is doing okay at handling herself around temptation?" Ask your group members to pick temptations that are particularly difficult to face. Then, talk together about how to run from, resist, or avoid them. Remember that Lot resisted leaving the city of Sodom, even with all its sin. We all have difficulty with the temptations we face. For Lot the two angels had to force him to leave the city.

5. You may get resistance from your group members on this exercise since they will not necessarily think these are things from which they need to be rescued. Talk about the need to be vigilant against temptation so that it won't get the best of you.

THE CLOSE

God gives us a toolbox full of tools to help us avoid sinful circumstances. It's our choice to use or not use these tools. We have Christian friends, our congregation, our parents, the Bible, the Holy Spirit. We can avoid, run, or resist the temptations that we all face. It's our choice.

Abraham Gets a Test

God turns our difficulties into faith-growing opportunities

1. Abraham obeyed God immediately. He got up early the next morning and prepared to give Isaac to God. When you hear God's word, the Bible, read at church or read the Bible yourself, how ready are you to obey God?

❏ Like Abraham, I'm ready to do whatever God asks of me.
❏ I'm ready to do most of what God asks of me.
❏ I'm ready to do a few of the things God asks of me.
❏ I'm not ready to obey God at all.

2. Abraham didn't let anything keep him from obeying God. What, if anything, is the biggest thing that keeps you from obeying God?

❏ Laziness   ❏ Stubbornness   ❏ Pride
❏ Jealousy/Envy   ❏ Greed   ❏ Anger
❏ Impatience   ❏ Hatred   ❏ Meanness
❏ Other: _____

3. Abraham traveled three long days to get to the place where God told him to go to sacrifice Isaac. Then, Abraham told his workers to wait for him and Isaac. Abraham knew by faith that God would spare Isaac's life and provide another sacrifice. He knew by faith that God always did what was right. He knew by faith that Isaac would not die that day. What would you have done if you were Abraham?

❏ I would have ignored God's request to sacrifice Isaac.
❏ I would have started on the journey to sacrifice Isaac but there is no way I would have trusted God for the three days like Abraham did.
❏ I would have taken the three-day journey but gone to the mountain without Isaac and pleaded with God.
❏ I would have done exactly what Abraham did.

On the third day Abraham looked up and saw the place in the distance. He said to his servants, "Stay here with the donkey while I and the boy go over there. We will worship and then we will come back to you."
(Genesis 22:4-5)

4. Abraham could have ignored the Lord and missed an opportunity to grow his faith. How often do you want to ignore God's faith-growing opportunities?

❏ All the time. I don't like difficult times.
❏ Most of the time.
❏ Some of the time.
❏ I don't want to ignore God's faith-growing opportunities. I look at the tough times in my life to see what God wants me to learn.

5. What do you do to ignore God?

❏ Skip reading my Bible   ❏ Avoid praying   ❏ Ditch Sunday school or Bible study
❏ Daydream during the worship service   ❏ Stay clear of friends who are Christians
❏ Other: _____

READ OUT LOUD

It was a strange request. God tells Abraham to kill his promised son. Weird. What was God trying to accomplish? Abraham's Canaanite neighbors practiced human sacrifice but that wasn't God's way. Had God changed? Did God now require human sacrifice to wipe away sin? No! Abraham had learned over a lifetime that God was trustworthy. The God who never changed had something else in mind for Abraham. It was a test—at test of Abraham's faithfulness. (Have a student read out loud the story found in Genesis 22:1-19—or have group members read it quietly to themselves.)

ASK

What is the hardest test you ever took?

DISCUSS, BY THE NUMBERS

1. First, talk about what messages your group members hear when they hear God's Word, the Bible, read at church or read the Bible themselves. Do they hear only a list of don'ts? Or do they hear the words of a loving God who wants the best for them? Now talk about their willingness to hear God's loving, protective words of life. Ask, "How is Abraham's immediate obedience a great example of how we should respond to God?"

2. Make a list of your group members' top three responses to the question, "What, if anything, is the biggest thing that keeps you from obeying God?" Now ask, "How do these responses keep you from obeying God?" Say something like, "These are the same responses that adults have to the question." Talk about ways to overcome these impediments to obedience.

3. It took Abraham a lifetime of living for God to get to this point of obedience in his life. Talk about where your group members are in their obedience to God. Say something like, "Living a life of faithful obedience to God is a journey with ups and downs. We need to continue to be part of a faith community—a church—to help us remain faithful to God."

4. Get a group consensus to answer the question, "How often do you want to ignore God's faith-growing opportunities?" Say something like, "None

of us like tough times, yet God can use them to grow our faith." Talk about a tough time in your life that God used to grow your faith. Encourage your group members to face life's difficulties with a desire to learn from them and grow in faith.

5. Your group members may not want to admit that they ignore God. But this exercise will help them see that, yes, sometimes they do. Talk about ways your group members can avoid ignoring God and practice the ways of faith—Bible reading, prayer, study, worship, fellowship.

THE CLOSE

God never wanted Abraham to kill his son Isaac as a sacrifice. Rather, God was teaching Abraham to completely surrender his life to him. Near the end of Abraham's life he proved to God that he truly had placed his trust in God. We too will be given opportunities to demonstrate our trust in Jesus Christ. Sometimes we may fail while other times we will succeed. The important thing for us to remember is that God will give us opportunities to grow in our faith. How we respond is up to us. God will always remain faithful. The challenge for us is to continue to rely on Jesus so that when difficult times arrive we are in the habit of trusting in God.

Dating... Old Testament Style

God wants a say in your romantic relationship choices

1. When it comes to getting serious with the opposite sex, a follower of Christ—

   ❏ should only get serious with other Christ-followers.
   ❏ should get serious with those they're attracted to.
   ❏ can do whatever they want.

2. Isaac was an adult when he met and married Rebekah. How old do you think people **should** be when they start to get involved in romantic relationships?

   (Circle one age.)
   10   11   12   13   14   15   16   17   18   19   20   21   22   older than 22

3. If you were to talk to an older Christian (other than your parents) who you respect about romantic relationships, to whom would you talk? What would you ask this person? What do you think they might say to you?

4. Abraham's employee prayed that God would find the right marriage partner for Isaac. I will pray that God will show me who I should date and marry.

   ❏ Absolutely
   ❏ Most likely
   ❏ Maybe
   ❏ Probably not
   ❏ No way

5. Amy sighed as she read the text. It was from Alex, her boyfriend of exactly one week. They were always texting each other or sending messages on Facebook®. Except for eating lunch together and seeing each other in English class it was the only time they got to talk. They only knew each other for two weeks before they decided to "go together" so they had a lot to talk about. Amy's parents would flip if they knew she had a boyfriend so she just didn't tell them. It was so much easier that way. Now Alex wanted her to meet him at the mall this weekend. Amy would have to figure out some sort of story to tell her parents so that she could get out of the house.

   What do you think of this relationship? What might God think?

READ OUT LOUD

Arranged marriages are foreign to Western culture. But the arranged marriages in the Old Testament can teach us a few things about Western dating. In today's story, Abraham is ready for his son Isaac to marry. The arrangements will be taken care of by one of Abraham's trusted employees. (Have a student read out loud the story found in Genesis 24:1-27—or have group members read it quietly to themselves.)

ASK

Do you think God has an opinion about dating? If so, do you want to know what that opinion is?

DISCUSS, BY THE NUMBERS

1. Read Genesis 24:3-4 out loud. The pagan cultures that surrounded Abraham were no place to find a wife for his son. He wanted Isaac to marry someone who believed in the one true God so he looked toward his roots for a suitable mate. We can infer from Abraham's situation that God wanted Isaac to be with a God-follower rather than someone who worshiped false gods or no god at all. In the New Testament, the Apostle Paul tells us to avoid involvement in intimate relationships (like dating) with unbelievers.

   "I want you to swear by the LORD, the God of heaven and the God of earth, that you will not get a wife for my son from the daughters of the Canaanites, among whom I am living, but will go to my country and my own relatives and get a wife for my son Isaac." (Genesis 24:3-4)

2. You'll get a range of responses here. Talk about the pros and cons of early dating and waiting until one is older. There are many dangers to getting involved with the opposite sex at a young age and many benefits to waiting until late high school or even college.

3. If you were to talk to an older Christian (other than your parents) who you respect about romantic relationships, to whom would you talk? What would you ask this person? What do you think they might say to you?

After examining your group members' answers to these questions, ask, "Do you think these people care about God's opinion concerning dating and marriage?"

4. Ask, "Why do you think we should pray for God's guidance in both dating and marriage?"

5. Explore all that is typical yet wrong with this situation. Ask something like, "Is it safe for Amy to be getting more involved with Alex?" "Should Amy keep this relationship from her parents?" "What do you think of Amy not consulting God about this relationship?"

THE CLOSE

Relationships are important to God. The relationship we have with God was so important that Jesus died to make it possible. God wants to be involved in your relationships. God wants the best for you so God tells us through today's Bible passage that we should not get involved in romantic relationships with unbelievers. And, of course, we must look at what is appropriate and inappropriate behavior when we do get involved in relationships with believers. God wants to protect you from all those things that can go wrong when we get involved with unbelievers or when we get too intimate with believers. Why not commit to dating only believers? Why not commit to date only those who you think God has chosen for you?

1. **Even though God could have easily taken Jacob, God chose to intentionally wrestle or interact with him. How does God intentionally interact with you?**

   ❑ God has concealed himself from me.
   ❑ God interacts with me through my questions.
   ❑ God connects with me through the Bible.
   ❑ God gets to me through prayer.
   ❑ God gets through to me through putting different people in my life.

The Big Wrestling Match

God gives us opportunities for new, exciting futures

2. **Jacob has encountered God and doesn't want to let God go until he gets some answers. What questions do you have for God? (Circle your biggest question.)**

   Why do such bad things happen in the world?
   Why are there mosquitoes?
   Do you really love me God?
   Did Jesus really die for my sins?
   Do you really hear my prayers?
   Why is there no blue food?
   Am I going to heaven?

3. **For Jacob to say his name to God ("Jacob, the deceiver") meant that he would be confessing his sinfulness to God.**

   ❑ I'm not that bad of a person. I don't need to tell God that I'm sinful.
   ❑ I've never confessed my sinfulness to God but need to.
   ❑ I've confessed my sinfulness to God but don't feel the forgiveness promised by Jesus.
   ❑ I've confessed my sinfulness to God and I have experienced Christ's forgiveness.

4. **Natalie looked at the seventh graders as they walked out of their "Welcome to Middle School" assembly. They looked so young! As a wiser, older eighth grader Natalie wondered if she really looked like that just last year. It seemed so long ago.** *I wish I could tell them a few things,* **thought Natalie. Seventh grade was so hard at first. There were some things that went on that she couldn't even tell her mom. Natalie was just glad that she had Jesus there with her to talk to. One Sunday her pastor said that God was big enough to handle anything if we just talked to him. So Natalie started talking.** *Maybe, that's what helped me get to be a different person than those seventh graders,* **she thought.**

   How had Jesus changed Natalie?

5. **Jacob received a new name from God. This gave Jacob a new identity. Jacob was a new person. God through Jesus Christ has given you a new and exciting future!**

   YES   YES   yes   ?   no   NO   NO

READ OUT LOUD

Today's story is weird. Told from Jacob's perspective, we find him preparing to meet his brother after 20 years. He is scared. His brother will probably kill him for his deception—stealing his blessing from their father. He sends his family ahead and hangs back alone. Then he encounters God in a wrestling match. (Have a student read out loud the story found in Genesis 32:22-32—or have group members read it quietly to themselves.)

ASK

In the future, will things be better or worse than they are today?

DISCUSS, BY THE NUMBERS

1. God, in human form, wrestled with Jacob. God chose to let this wrestling match go on all night even though God obviously could have taken Jacob out at any moment. God can't get away because he chose to remain with Jacob. God was intentionally interacting with Jacob for a spiritual reason. God wants to intentionally interact with you and your group members. Discuss the ways God interacts with us today—through prayer, our questions to God, through Bible study, through the people we encounter (in our congregation, in group Bible study, at school, in our family). God also interacts with us through the difficult situations we encounter in our lives. This is one your group members won't want to hear.

2. Use this exercise as an opportunity to discuss the tough questions your group members have asked God. Perhaps they have never been given an answer. You may not have the answers either but don't back away from your group members' doubts or frustrations with God. It's time to wrestle. And sometimes we don't get answers from God. "Why do such bad things happen in the world? Why are there mosquitoes? Do you really love me God? Did Jesus really die for my sins? Do you really hear my prayers? Why is there no blue food? Am I going to heaven?"

3. For Jacob to say his name to God ("Jacob, the deceiver") meant that he was confessing his sinfulness to God. Names meant something more

in the Old Testament than they do today. When Jacob spoke his name to God he confessed his brokenness and need for God. He repented! Use this exercise to explore your group's desire to confess their sinfulness before God. While they may not have committed sins that, to them, aren't so horrible, they need to recognize that *any* sin separates humans from God.

4. Explore the contrived situation with your group, talking about how Jesus didn't rescue Natalie from her situation but helped her through it. Talk about how God has changed, is changing, and will continue to change your group members through his grace.

5. Explore how Jesus makes life exciting. Like Jacob, God gives us second chances again and again and again. Ask, "How do you take advantage of God's second chances?"

THE CLOSE

Does your life sometimes seem like a wrestling match? Don't give up. Keep on keeping on. Jesus is there for you. He wants to give you a new life, an exciting life! You'll never have a dull moment in life if you choose to continue following Christ. His purpose for you may be unclear in the details. But the big picture is to make you into a new person. Jesus wants to give your past a new meaning and to give you a future that has meaning as well. Just trust him!

Esau Forgives Jacob

Two parts to forgiveness

1. *Forgive* in the Greek means to let go of a sin as if the person had never done it. How easy is it for you to forgive others who have wronged you?

❏ Really easy
❏ Sort of easy
❏ Sort of difficult
❏ Impossible

2. Esau gave Jacob a big forgiving hug.

	Parent	Brother/Sister	Friend	Teacher	Coach
Who has forgiven you?	❏ Parent	❏ Brother/Sister	❏ Friend	❏ Teacher	❏ Coach
Who have you forgiven?	❏ Parent	❏ Brother/Sister	❏ Friend	❏ Teacher	❏ Coach

3. Esau cried as he hugged Jacob, demonstrating his complete forgiveness of his brother.

I need to be completely forgiven by God because—

4. What are the possible roadblocks to you forgiving someone else?

❏ I want revenge.
❏ I'm too angry to forgive.
❏ They don't deserve forgiveness.
❏ I hate them.
❏ It's not fair for them to get forgiveness.
❏ Other: _____

5. Check the box after each statement that best describes you.

	ALWAYS	MOSTLY	SOMETIMES	NEVER
I can accept God's forgiveness of all my sins.	❏	❏	❏	❏
I can forgive but I can't forget the hurt others did to me.	❏	❏	❏	❏
To be forgiven I must allow someone to forgive me.	❏	❏	❏	❏
I'm not sure Christ has forgiven me for my sins.	❏	❏	❏	❏
I don't always deserve to be forgiven.	❏	❏	❏	❏

READ OUT LOUD

Jacob was heading home after a 20-year absence. Why? God told him to go home. So Jacob loads up the family RV and heads for Canaan. But he was troubled by one thing. At home was Esau, who Jacob had cheated out of his birthright. When Jacob had left home Esau had threatened to kill him. Today's story is a story of forgiveness, both accepting it and giving it. (Have a student read out loud the story from Genesis 33:1-15—or have group members read it quietly to themselves.)

ASK

Which of your toys would you not forgive someone for playing with when you were a kid?

DISCUSS, BY THE NUMBERS

1. Even though God forgives us for all of our wrongdoing, it can be tough for us to be forgivers. Forgiveness is a big deal. We too often take God's forgiveness for granted yet find it sometimes impossible to forgive others. Ask, "Why do you think it is so tough to forgive others who have wronged us even though we have experienced God's forgiveness of our sins?"

2. Talk about the difference between forgiveness and reconciliation. We can forgive someone but not be reconciled to the person who wronged us. For example, in the case of sexual assault, the victim can forgive the assailant without being the assailant's friend.

3. Explore with your group what it means to truly be forgiven by God—your sins are separated from you as far as the east is from the west (Psalm 103:12). Young people in middle school often wrestle with feelings of guilt because of all the changes through which their bodies and minds are going. They will say and do things that they quickly regret. Help them examine the forgiveness that is available to them through Jesus Christ.

4. Discuss each of the possible roadblocks, talking about why these issues so easily block our forgiving others. Ask your group to imagine what might happen if these roadblocks affected God's forgiveness of us. It doesn't take much imagination to realize that God wouldn't forgive any of us. But fortunately, God doesn't act like us. And God has called us to be forgivers like God has forgiven us. Recite the Lord's Prayer and you quickly realize that we are called to forgive others as God has forgiven us (Matthew 6:12).

5. Being forgiven is a difficult thing. To truly accept forgiveness there are some things that have to happen. First, you have to acknowledge that you have done something wrong. This is more than simply taking the blame, or admitting a mistake. This is a deep-down in your inner-self willingness to acknowledge that you've done something, with no excuses. Second, you have to fully accept the consequences of that mistake, which means understanding the full impact of what you have done. You have to really understand the hurt you have caused, and that's a painful thing to do.

   And finally, you need to empty yourself of yourself. This is the hard one. You can be sorry about something that you have done, but mostly because of what it means to or about yourself. But to really accept forgiveness you have to stop thinking about yourself, and open your heart to the pain of someone else.

THE CLOSE

Esau and Jacob teach us that forgiveness requires two miracles. The first is forgiving. This is what Esau did with Jacob. He forgave him. But today's story was more about Jacob than Esau which brings us to the second miracle of forgiveness—accepting the forgiveness that is offered to us. We are forgiven and then we must allow that forgiveness to enter our lives. We must acknowledge our wrongdoing, accept the consequences of our wrongdoing, and put aside our pride.

So are you willing and able to forgive others and are you willing and able to accept the forgiveness offered you?

Joseph "For Sale"

God is with us, even on the roller coaster of family life

1. Joseph's brothers weren't happy with him. They fought over what to do about him. Which of the following ways does your family use to make up after a disagreement? Place a check mark by your answers.

___ Make up?
___ Say I'm sorry.
___ Not speak for days.
___ Have a family meeting.
___ Give each other a hug and say "I love you."
___ Mope around the house.
___ Take responsibility for your actions.
___ Not forgive or forget.
___ Not talk about it again and pretend it never happened.
___ Hope someone else gets in trouble so the focus will be off you.

2. Circle the best answer to the question, "How difficult is it to obey your parents?"

The hardest thing ever.
Not too hard when I want to.
Really hard because I have to admit I am wrong.
Not hard at all.

3. Joseph was always letting his father, Jacob, know about the bad things his brothers had done. Label each statement with a TAT* (for tattling) or TEL* (for telling).

*Tattling is trying to get someone into trouble. Telling is trying to get someone help to get out of trouble.
___ Your sister hits you in the arm while walking by you. You holler for your mom.
___ Your brother is smoking marijuana. You say something to your dad.
___ Your sister is letting passengers drive with her against your parents' wishes. You inform your parents.
___ A friend gives away your secret to a mutual friend.
___ The teacher's pet accuses you of cheating on a math test.
___ Your best friend talks about committing suicide. You go to the school counselor.
___ Your sister is hanging out with a "party" crowd. You say something to your mom.

4. God can do nothing about the bad things that happen in families.

❏ Strongly agree   ❏ Agree   ❏ Disagree   ❏ Strongly disagree

5. Joseph and his family weren't getting along at all. Think about the last time you weren't getting along with your family. Which of the following did you try?

❏ Talked to God   ❏ Talked to my friends   ❏ Talked to another caring adult
❏ Talked to my parents ❏ Didn't talk at all   ❏ Other: _____

READ OUT LOUD

Joseph, out of obedience to his father Jacob, traveled to check on his brothers' well-being. As sheep ranchers they grazed their flocks on public lands many miles away from home. Told to report back to his father, Joseph went off unaware that the hatred his brothers had for him because of their father's favoritism would change his life forever. (Have a student read out loud the story from Genesis 37:12-36—or have group members read it quietly to themselves.)

ASK

How do you act toward family members when you are mad at them?

DISCUSS, BY THE NUMBERS

1. Use this exercise to begin a conversation on how your group's family members handle disagreements. This will open the group up to talk more about family life as you move through the TalkSheet.

2. You will most likely get a wide range of responses because families differ greatly on how they function. Talk about the benefits of obeying parents even though there are times when parent requests seem impossible. Ask, "Is there ever a time you should not obey your parents or grandparents? How do you think God might help you do a better job of obeying your parents and grandparents?"

3. Begin by talking about the difference between "tattling" and "telling."

   Tattling is trying to get someone into trouble. Telling is trying to get someone help to get out of trouble. Ask, "Do you think Joseph was 'tattling' or 'telling'?" Go through each statement, letting your group members decide if the situation is tattling or telling. Ask, "What would God want you to do in each of these situations?"

4. Our fallen, sinful world is filled with evil. This is not God's fault but humankind's. God can, however, work through evil circumstances to create good. In Joseph's time this was true; God worked within his dysfunctional family situation to produce good. The same is true in today's families. When we rely on Jesus Christ, he will take bad situations and use them for good.

5. Use this exercise to talk about God's involvement in our families no matter how healthy or dysfunctional.

THE CLOSE

Joseph's brothers meant to harm Joseph but God turned the tragedy into something good. God was present with Joseph throughout his ordeal. Joseph may have wondered where God was throughout his time of hardship. But he stuck by God because he knew God was stuck to him. Through the good times and the bad in our family lives, we can count on God being with us.

The Lord Is with Joseph

How does it show that Jesus is with you?

1. The Lord was with Joseph.

Is the Lord with you?
❑ Yes ❑ No ❑ I don't know
Has Jesus made you different?
❑ Yes ❑ No ❑ I don't know
Can others see the difference?
❑ Yes ❑ No ❑ I don't know

2. How old should a person be before they are allowed to hang out one-on-one with the opposite sex?

_____ At the mall together?
_____ On a car date?
_____ At the movies together?
_____ In your bedroom with the door open?
_____ In your bedroom with the door closed?
_____ At a friend's house, no parents?
_____ In a Jacuzzi together, no one else?

3. Potiphar's wife would have a "reputation" today for being promiscuous (sex with a number of people). How does each of the following affect a young person's reputation?

Ways of dancing—
Clothes—
Body language—
Friends—
Musical taste—

4. I can handle the temptations that come my way.

YES   YES   yes   ?   no   NO   NO

5. "I can't believe that you just did that!" said Katie as she spun around to glare at William. William had just snapped her bra as they walked out of class.

"What?" asked William, trying to act all innocent.

"You know what," said Katie. "You should keep your hands to yourself, William."

"Or what?" asked William. He didn't really take Katie's threat very seriously.

Katie slugged him hard in the arm. She really wasn't a violent person but William had been doing this to her friends too and she'd had enough.

"Ow!" said William.

"If I even see you try to do that again I'm going to tell my friends to punch you, too!" said Katie as she walked to her next class.

What do you think of the way Katie handled the situation with William?

READ OUT LOUD

Potiphar purchased Joseph from slave traders who had traveled to Egypt. Remember that his brothers sold him into slavery. Potiphar could tell that there was something special about Joseph—that Joseph's God was with him. With Joseph in charge of Potiphar's household, Potiphar prospered. Potiphar's wife also had plans for Joseph. (Have a student read out loud the story from Genesis 39:1-20—or have group members read it quietly to themselves.)

ASK

Are you capable of talking maturely about sex?

DISCUSS, BY THE NUMBERS

Note to Leader: Remember, that some of your group members may have already gone farther than kissing, perhaps some have had sexual intercourse. Be sensitive and compassionate as you lead your group into a faith conversation about sex.

1. Read Genesis 39:2 out loud. What Potiphar saw in Joseph was a reflection of God. Since Joseph was a God-follower, the Holy Spirit had been molding Joseph into a new creation. Lead a faith conversation about how those who aren't followers of Christ see Christ-followers as distinct from other people in a good way. Some followers of Christ do give Christians a bad name but we can't do much about them. Tell a story of how Jesus has made you different and how that difference has been noticed by others. Encourage your group members to let Jesus shine through them so that their friends and family see the difference.

> *The LORD was with Joseph so that he prospered, and he lived in the house of his Egyptian master. (Genesis 39:2)*

2. Use Joseph as an example of a God-follower who stayed away from Potiphar's wife. The biblical principle is you can choose to avoid putting yourself in tempting situations. Ask, "How does being alone with the opposite sex place you in tempting situations as you get older?" Tell stories about yourself or friends who needed to be warned in middle school about coming temptations like sex in order to avoid them.

3. Talk together about how each of the following affects a young person's reputation:
   • Ways of dancing
   • Clothes
   • Body language
   • Friends
   • Musical taste

4. Explore with your group members regarding how best they think they can handle the temptations that come their way. Read Genesis 39:10. Say something like, "Joseph had two strategies. First, he refused Potiphar's wife. Second, he tried to stay away from Potiphar's wife. You can do the same—say no when you are in a tempting situation and stay away from tempting situations when you can."

> *And though she spoke to Joseph day after day, he refused to go to bed with her or even be with her. (Genesis 39:10)*

5. Use this situation to answer three questions: What do you think of William's actions? What do you think of Katie's handling of the situation with William? Do you think an adult should be told about what William did?

THE CLOSE

Why was sexual purity important to Joseph? Joseph was a person who put God first in his life. More than anything else Joseph desired to be friends with God; to please God in all he did. Is sexual purity important to you? Do you want to put God first in your life? Do you want to be friends with God; to please God in all you do? No matter what you've thought, said, or done in the past, it's never too late to put a high priority on your sexual purity so that you put God first in your life before anything else, including sex.

No Ordinary Joe

God is shaping us for leadership in our congregation and community

1. Young people my age are much lazier than Joseph.

❑ I agree ❑ I disagree ❑ I'm not sure

2. Joseph was ready at a young age to take on more and more responsibility. At what age do you think people should be to take on new responsibilities at church? On the line before each statement, write the age a person should be to do the task.

_____ Serve Communion
_____ Sit on the church board
_____ Teach Sunday school
_____ Sing in the choir/member of worship band
_____ Work in the church kitchen
_____ Lead prayer
_____ Read Scripture during worship
_____ Preach a sermon
_____ Greet/usher
_____ Lead a small group Bible study
_____ Preach a sermon

3. How often do you think Joseph prayed about his responsibilities?

❑ Often ❑ Sometimes ❑ Rarely

How often do you think he prayed for wisdom?

❑ Often ❑ Sometimes ❑ Rarely

How often do you pray for more responsibilities?

❑ Often ❑ Sometimes ❑ Rarely

4. Circle the top five most important characteristics of a great leader.

Compassionate	Forward-looking	Loving	Good looking	Competent	Organized
Even-tempered	Fair	Team player	Patient	Christ-follower	Confident
Fun loving	Peace maker	Assertive	Honest	Inspiring	Intelligent
Forgiving	Understanding	Determined	Other: _____		

"And now let Pharaoh look for a discerning and wise man and put him in charge of the land of Egypt."
(Genesis 41:33)

5. Joseph was a leader over Egypt. Where do you lead?

❑ Home ❑ Church ❑ School ❑ Sports Team ❑ Community

God calls us to be faithful, not successful. You may fail, but you are not a failure.

READ OUT LOUD

Joseph, having been falsely accused of sexual assault by Potiphar's wife, was languishing in prison. Pharaoh's personal servant, who had done time in prison with Joseph, suggested that Joseph be summoned to interpret the Pharaoh's strange dreams. Joseph was pulled out of prison and correctly interpreted the dreams. The dreams predicted seven years of abundance followed by seven years of famine for Egypt. (Have a student read out loud the story found in Genesis 41:33-57—or have group members read it quietly to themselves.)

ASK

When was the last time a parent or teacher said "act your age"?

DISCUSS, BY THE NUMBERS

1. Talk about ways your group members could demonstrate that they are ready to take on more responsibilities at home and in the congregation. Why is this important? God is shaping them to be leaders. And to be leaders they must take on more responsibility as they mature. One mark of maturity is leadership.

2. Compare the ages suggested by different group members. See if you can arrive at a group consensus. Ask, "What are you willing to do at church to demonstrate to adults that you can handle more responsibilities?"

3. Use this exercise to help you talk about prayer as an important component of leadership. God uses prayer to talk with you and shape you into the leader he wants you to become.

4. Read Genesis 41:33 out loud. Make a group list of the characteristics of a great leader. Ask, "Which of the characteristics found on the TalkSheet describe what it means to be a Christian?"

   Compassionate
   Forward-looking
   Loving
   Good looking
   Competent
   Organized
   Even-tempered
   Fair
   Team player
   Patient
   Christ-follower
   Confident
   Fun loving
   Peace maker
   Assertive
   Honest
   Inspiring
   Intelligent
   Forgiving
   Understanding
   Determined
   Other: _____

"And now let Pharaoh look for a discerning and wise man and put him in charge of the land of Egypt." (Genesis 41:33)

5. God is working to shape each of your group members as a member of the body of Christ to fulfill his purposes in the kingdom. Wherever you find yourselves leading (even if you don't find yourselves leading all that much right now), you can be confident that God is always moving you toward being effective leaders in some way.

THE CLOSE

Joseph's life looked clearer near the end rather than when he was younger. Our lives are no different. Some things are clearer from the rearview mirror. If we only read the stories from the beginning of Joseph's life—sold into slavery; thrown into prison for sexual assault—we would see only hardship and misfortune. But we have the advantage of seeing the big picture. We can look back and see how God worked through the circumstances in his life to further God's kingdom. Joseph continued to be obedient to God and do the tasks that were before him no matter how difficult or ugly things became in his life. Can the same be said of our lives? Can we keep on doing the tasks God has placed before us? Can we keep talking with our friends about Jesus? Can we keep doing our best in school? Can we keep working to make our family life the best that it can be? God knows the big picture. *". . . for it is God who works in you to will and to act in order to fulfill his good purpose." (Philippians 2:13)*

God's People Aren't Immune to Suffering . . . Even Miserably

But hardship can mature and strengthen your faith

1. God used the suffering inflicted by the Egyptians to strengthen the faith of the Jews. What does God use to help strengthen your faith?

   ❏ My parents
   ❏ Conflict with friends
   ❏ Suffering at school
   ❏ A tragedy that happened to me
   ❏ My church
   ❏ Adults who push me to do well
   ❏ Other: _____

2. God allowed the Jews to suffer under the rule of the Egyptians. God will allow you to suffer, too. How will you respond when suffering invades your world?

   ❏ I'll be angry with God.
   ❏ I won't handle it well.
   ❏ I'll be a crybaby.
   ❏ I'll be joyful.
   ❏ I'll try to learn from it.
   ❏ I'll cry out to God for help.
   ❏ I'll find relief by smoking marijuana.
   ❏ I'll talk with an adult I trust.

3. How many of the Jews do you think rejected God because of their suffering?

   ❏ None of them   ❏ Only a few of them   ❏ Some of them   ❏ Most of them   ❏ All of them

4. (Circle all that apply.) Suffering helps you—

   a. see the glass half empty.
   b. get a bad attitude.
   c. learn to rely totally on Jesus.
   d. become more self-centered.

5. What do you think comforted God's suffering people while they lived in Egypt?

   ❏ Experiencing God's presence
   ❏ Seeing the pyramids
   ❏ Kayaking the Nile River
   ❏ God's people comforting each other with God's promises
   ❏ Approaching God in prayer
   ❏ Walking like an Egyptian

READ OUT LOUD

Joseph and his extended family had all died. The Israelites had not returned to the land of Canaan, modern-day Israel, but had prospered in Egypt. Now a new Pharaoh was in power—a ruler who had no idea what Joseph had done for Egypt. He was worried that the Israelites would take over Egypt. His solution? Enslave the Israelites. Keep them in submission to the Egyptians. Control what they do. And try to reduce their population. (Have a student read out loud the story found in Exodus 1:6-22—or have group members read it quietly to themselves.)

ASK

What subject could you take a test in right now and get an A+?

DISCUSS, BY THE NUMBERS

1. Throughout the Bible God used suffering to strengthen his people. Ask, "Why do you think it takes suffering for our faith to get stronger?" Talk about the different things God has used to strengthen the faith of your group members.
   - My parents
   - Conflict with friends
   - Suffering at school
   - A tragedy that happened to me
   - My church
   - Adults who push me to do well
2. Many, many Bible passages guarantee that we will suffer. James 1:2-4 tells us how we ought to respond. (And remember: Those who aren't followers of Christ will also suffer—without the presence of Christ to walk through the suffering with them.)

   Consider it pure joy, my brothers and sisters, whenever you face trials of many kinds, because you know that the testing of your faith produces perseverance. Let perseverance finish its work so that you may be mature and complete, not lacking anything.
   (James 1:2-4)

3. Talk about how the suffering of the Hebrews under the Pharaoh could have pushed some of them away from God while drawing others close to God. Then discuss the effect suffering has had on your

group members. Don't discount their stories of suffering as petty. Suffering for a young person may be perceived differently by them than by an adult.

4. Suffering can put our faith to the test. If we see suffering as an opportunity to grow in our faith, then it can help us learn to rely totally on Jesus. The more we trust in Jesus the more we will trust in Jesus!
5. Talk about each of the ways your group members think that God's suffering people were comforted while they lived in Egypt. They most likely 1) experienced God's presence; 2) comforted each other with God's promises; and 3) approached God in prayer.

Note: It seems as though the nurses—Shiphrah and Puah (probably head nurses)—lied to Pharaoh. The nurses refused to kill the Hebrew babies. The pregnant Hebrew women were required to work hard as slaves up to the time of the delivery of their babies. They were in great physical shape which helped accelerate their time in labor. This would explain why the nurses were unable to get to them in time to kill their male children. The Hebrew women could have birthed their male children and had the time to hide them before any of the nurses arrived to assist in the delivery and then kill the male children. This being true, the nurses didn't need to lie to Pharaoh. The slavery that Pharaoh meant as evil turned out to make the birthing process easier for the Israelite women.

THE CLOSE

Everyone suffers whether you are a believer or unbeliever. While suffering does put our faith to the test, we can use suffering as an opportunity to grow in our reliance on Christ.

The Birth of Moses

God guides our life circumstances

1. Is your family more like Moses' family or more un-like his family?

   ❏ My family is more like Moses' family.
   ❏ My family is more unlike Moses' family.

2. God used the Pharaoh's daughter, a woman who worshiped the false gods of Egypt, to save Moses' life. If God can use her for his purposes he most certainly can use you. Do you want God to work through you for his purposes?

   ❏ Absolutely
   ❏ Possibly
   ❏ Not at all

3. God was directing the life of baby Moses and—

   ❏ God is directing my life all of the time.
   ❏ God is directing my life most of the time.
   ❏ God is directing my life some of the time.
   ❏ God is never directing my life.

4. Moses would have heard the story of his birth by the time he was an adult living in Pharaoh's court. How can the faith stories in the Bible help strengthen your faith?

   ❏ I can see that the characters in the Bible are just like me.
   ❏ The Bible stories are pretend stories so they can't really help me.
   ❏ Like me the characters in the Bible struggled with sin.
   ❏ The characters in the Bible can show me how to rely on God.
   ❏ The Bible stories are boring and I can't get anything out of them.

5. Natalie was so excited. It had been hard to make friends at her new school. But today, two of the most popular girls at school asked Natalie to go to a concert with them. Okay, so some of their songs had some pretty raw lyrics, but they were so popular! Natalie couldn't believe it when she called her mom to tell her about it and her mom said no!

   How could this be an example of God using Mom for Natalie's own good?

6. Moses probably had the opportunity to get together with his birth family to visit and talk. Do you think they talked about the false gods Moses learned about while with Pharaoh's family? Do you think they talked about their faith in the God of the Bible?

READ OUT LOUD

There was a death sentence given for all male babies. That's why, in today's story, Moses was kept inside for the first three months of his life. His older brother Aaron and his older sister Miriam missed the Pharaoh's death sentence.

The Bible tells us that Moses was a beautiful baby, which is probably why Pharaoh's daughter rescued him from the waters of the Nile. It's fascinating to consider that Pharaoh wanted all the male Hebrew babies dead yet ended up the adopted grandfather of the baby who would rescue the Israelites from slavery. (Have a student read out loud the story found in Exodus 2:1-10—or have group members read it quietly to themselves.)

ASK

How good are you at giving directions?

DISCUSS, BY THE NUMBERS

1. Moses' mother did everything she could to keep him alive. Moses' sister helped rescue and raise Moses. Moses' family was a family of faith. Talk about the similarities and differences in Moses' family and the families of your group members. Ask, "How can your faith make a positive difference in your family?"

2. What an amazing story. Our God ordered events so that Pharaoh's daughter spared Moses' life. The Pharaoh who wanted all the Hebrew baby boys dead ended up paying for Moses' education in the royal household. Since God could use the Pharaoh's daughter, a woman who worshiped the false gods of Egypt, to save Moses' life, God can use your group members for his purposes as well. Talk about your group members' willingness to be used by God. Ask, "How have you seen God work in the lives of others your age?"

3. Today's big idea, that God guides the circumstances in our lives, can be seen in today's story and throughout the Bible. With that said, it is also true that our sin and our choices can go against what God has for us. We can choose to turn our lives over to God or attempt to live life through our own efforts. Discuss what a life given over to Christ looks like versus a life lived by one's own efforts.

4. See commentary in bold:
   - I can see that the characters in the Bible are just like me. **Talk about how you see yourself in the Bible stories. This is an opportunity for you to make the stories real for your group members. Ask, "How are the characters in the Bible like you?"**
   - The Bible stories are pretend stories so they can't really help me. **This is your chance to talk about the inspiration of Scripture. God superintended the writing of the Bible. The stories are true which is why they can be trusted.**
   - Like me the characters in the Bible struggled with sin. **They certainly did. We can see the reality of sin and the power of God working through Bible characters.**
   - The characters in the Bible can show me how to rely on God. **In the lives of Bible characters we see examples of trusting in God or turning away from God and its consequences.**
   - The Bible stories are boring and I can't get anything out of them. **If your group members see them as boring, then something has gone wrong in their Christian education.**

5. Use this situation to start a faith conversation about how God works through the circumstances of our lives, even tragedies, to work his will. While God doesn't cause the evil in our world (sin does that), God does guide the circumstances in our lives. This is called providence.

6. Talking with our family members about Jesus and faith issues can help strengthen our relationship with Christ. Discuss with your group members about ways they can talk more with their families about their faith in Christ.

THE CLOSE

While we don't always see God working behind the scenes for our benefit, God is there superintending the situations in our lives. This doesn't mean God causes the sinful things that happen to us. Our fallen (sinful) world creates horrendous evil. That is the fault of our own sins, others' sins, and satanic influence in our fallen world. But in spite of evil, God is at work to ensure that his will is done. Let's turn our life and our wills over to Christ so that we intentionally cooperate with God as he directs our life circumstances.

Moses Loses His Cool

We can run from our problems—
or we can run to God

1. Moses was a God-follower. He chose the God of the Bible over the fake gods of the Egyptians. Are you a Christ-follower?

   ❑ Yes   ❑ No   ❑ Maybe

2. If you are a Christ-follower, how much time do you spend with God's people?

   ❑ Very little time   ❑ Enough time
   ❑ Lots of time   ❑ Too much time

3. **Question Blitz:** Everyone has problems. And everyone likes to run away from those problems. Moses was no exception. How are your problems just like the problems of other young people your age? How are they different? Do you think the adults you know had similar problems to yours when they were your age? How ready are you to give your problems to God?

4. Moses ran from his problem. How do you think Christ wants us to handle our problems?

   ❑ Run away from them.
   ❑ Pretend there are no problems.
   ❑ Forget about them.
   ❑ Share our problems with him and with his people, the church.
   ❑ Attend church every week so the problems will go away.

5. How could Joe tell his mom that he broke his glasses again? He just got a new pair three weeks ago. His mom told him then that with money so tight she couldn't afford for him to be so careless with his glasses. All right, so that time he sat on them. But this time it wasn't his fault; he was minding his own business at lunch when a ball hit the side of his head.

   Maybe they could just be straightened out, he thought as he looked at the mangled frames. Okay, so maybe not. He would just have to go without them for a few weeks and then tell his mom.

   How is he running from his problem? What should he do? How can Jesus help?

READ OUT LOUD

Moses is now 40 years old (Acts 7:23). Having grown up with the opportunities and luxuries afforded by living in the Pharaoh's household, he wishes to help his people, the Israelites. He ventures out of his comfort zone and sees the suffering the Israelites are experiencing. He encounters an Egyptian who is harshly beating a Hebrew slave. We can surmise that the Egyptian beat the Hebrew slave to death. Moses reacts by killing the Egyptian, an act that was justified under Hebrew law. The Pharaoh finds out and Moses goes on the run. (Have a student read out loud the whole story from Exodus 2:11-21—or have group members read it quietly to themselves.)

ASK

If you could outrun an animal, what could you beat?

DISCUSS, BY THE NUMBERS

1. Moses was raised by his family until he was older. Then he lived with his adopted mom, the daughter of the Egyptian Pharaoh. He was a God-follower as an adult. Moses was most likely influenced by his Hebrew family and was well aware of his heritage of belonging to God's chosen people. Even though he was raised into adulthood in Pharaoh's household with its worship of multiple gods, Moses was a God-follower as an adult. Ask, "What does it mean to be a Christ-follower?" "What responsibilities does a Christ-follower have to Jesus? To her or his family? To a congregation? To a community?" "What do you like most about being a follower of Jesus?"

2. This is the opportunity to talk about the importance of a congregation in supporting our Christian growth. Talk about how one's involvement in the life of the congregation can help your group members grow. Discuss how your congregation can help them solve life's problems together.

3. Talk about your group members' responses to the questions. Use this as an opportunity to discuss how Christians can handle problems differently than unbelievers because of Jesus.

4. The answer is the fourth option. Running away from them, pretending that we don't have problems or forgetting them won't solve our problems. Also, church attendance is no guarantee that all our problems will go away. Moses ran from his problem and spent the next 40 years living in the desert. Why not practice giving our problems to Jesus and to God's people? Running to God and his people instead of away from problems is the best solution.

5. Use this situation to talk practically about how best to handle problems. Ask, "How many people do what Joe does when they have a problem to solve?" "How does trying to escape our problems only make them worse?"

THE CLOSE

While the easy answer is to run as fast as possible from our problems, doing so only makes them worse. Moses found this out the hard way. He spent 40 years in the desert. We need to learn how to face our problems head on with God's help instead of running from them.

Moses Checks Out a Burning Bush

God sees what we need and provides for us

1. God heard the cry for help of God's people living in Egypt. Do you think God hears your cries for help?

- ❏ All of the time
- ❏ Most of the time
- ❏ Some of the time
- ❏ Never

2. A burning bush that didn't burn up got Moses to pay attention to God. What does God use to grab your attention?

- ❏ My mom or dad grounding me
- ❏ Feeling guilty
- ❏ A bad thing happens to me or someone else
- ❏ Adults at my church who talk with me about something important
- ❏ When I feel sad
- ❏ When I read a Bible story or verse
- ❏ Other: _____

3. As Jason sat listening to the sermon he wondered how someone his age could do all the great things for God that the pastor was challenging the congregation to do. It just didn't seem like there was anything he could do. It was really frustrating. Sure, he heard all about how he was supposed to "witness" to his friends, but come on, who does that? He tried it once, it wasn't pretty. *I guess I'll just wait 'til I get older*, Jason thought. *Maybe then it will be easier.*

Jason felt unqualified to be used by God. When do you usually feel inadequate, incompetent, or somehow insufficient to be used by God?

4. Moses was used by God to save God's people suffering in Egypt. How could God use you to help others?

- ❏ I could talk with my friends about Jesus.
- ❏ I could volunteer with a friend to help out at a soup kitchen.
- ❏ I could tell residents of a nursing home about God's love.
- ❏ I could help someone at school.
- ❏ I'm too afraid to help others.
- ❏ Other: _____

5. Moses listened to God and responded by saying, "Here I am" (Exodus 3:4b). How do you respond to Christ?

- ❏ I'm not here. And please don't look for me.
- ❏ Here I am. I want a relationship with you but I don't want to do anything for you.
- ❏ Here I am. I'll do some of the things you want me to do.
- ❏ Here I am. I'll do anything you want me to do.

READ OUT LOUD

Moses knew 40 years ago that God would use him to free the Israelites from their slavery under Egyptian rule (see Acts 7:23-25). He himself ran from Egypt 40 years ago and probably had let go of his dream to help his people. But after 40 years God is again ready to use him to free the Israelites. Moses encounters God in a burning bush. God announces that he has heard the cries for help out of Egypt. God has seen what his people need and will provide a way of escape through Moses. (Have a student read out loud the story found in Exodus 3:1-15—or have group members read it quietly to themselves.)

ASK

What toppings do you most need on your pizza? What kind of drink do you most need on a hot day?

DISCUSS, BY THE NUMBERS

1. God has always been there for his people, whether it was during the time of Moses or today. God hears our cries for help. But we can't expect to get the answer we think is best when we do beg God for help. God is all-powerful and will do what is best for our situation and the growth of our faith.

2. Perhaps your group members have never considered that God is trying to get their attention through "getting grounded" or "adults talking with them." Use this time to discuss together the importance of listening for God's voice in all kinds of situations.

3. Moses felt unqualified to be used by God. But God saw what Moses needed and provided Aaron to help. Jason felt unqualified to be used by God. Explore the question, "When do you usually feel inadequate, incompetent, or somehow insufficient to be used by God?" with your group. Ask, "How willing are you to surrender your will to God's so that God can meet your inadequacies?"

4. Explore other possible and practical ways in which your group members could help others. Talk about a possible service project that your group would be willing to do together.

5. Use this exercise to talk about your group members' commitment to Christ. Like Jesus called the disciples, he is calling each of your group members to follow him. But they have a choice. Will they follow him completely? Will they commit all of themselves to him? Tell stories of your faith journey—how your commitment to Christ has grown as you have followed him. Read Ephesians 3:20-21 out loud. Use this passage to discuss together the power that is available to us through Christ when we live for him.

Now to him who is able to do immeasurably more than all we ask or imagine, according to his power that is at work within us, to him be glory in the church and in Christ Jesus throughout all generations, for ever and ever! Amen. (Ephesians 3:20-21)

THE CLOSE

The Israelites begged God for help. They desperately wanted God to rescue them from their slavery in Egypt. God heard their cries for help and sent Moses to liberate them. God is a big God who sees what we need and provides for us.

Moses Makes Excuses

What's the point of making excuses to the One who knows the truth?

1. Moses was afraid to speak for God. What scares you the most?

❑ To talk with a friend or acquaintance about Jesus
❑ To pray in public
❑ To speak in front of others at a Bible study
❑ To read the Bible in front of others
❑ To go up front to do something during a worship service
❑ To teach a Sunday school class or small group

2. Moses made excuses to God about his speaking abilities. What excuse do you usually use to get you out of doing something for God?

❑ I'm too scared to do it.　　❑ I don't know enough about the Bible.　　❑ I don't know how to do it.
❑ I'm too busy.　　❑ There are others more qualified than me.　　❑ I wouldn't be good at it.

3. Moses finally said yes to God. When God asked you to do something, what do you usually say?

❑ God has never asked me to do anything.　　❑ I usually resist what God asked me to do.
❑ I usually do what God asks me to do.　　❑ I'm always confused about what God wants me to do.

4. "So do you go to church?" asked Sandra.

Abby had been sitting with her at lunch for the last few days, you know, just trying to be friendly. Then this happened. Abby went to church but she didn't go around telling everyone about it. Then her pastor talked about how God sometimes puts the opportunity to share right there in front of you so you can't ignore it. Abby had a funny feeling that this was one of those times.

Come on Lord, thought Abby. *I'm not ready for this. I don't know what to say. What if I mess up and scare her away from church completely?*

What do you think of Abby's response to God? How often do you think like Abby?

5. God has been patient with me just like God was with Moses.

❑ Yes, God has been patient with me.　　❑ No, God has not been patient with me.　　❑ I'm not sure.

6. Are you as stubborn as Moses was with God?

❑ More stubborn than Moses　　❑ About as stubborn as Moses　　❑ Less stubborn than Moses

READ OUT LOUD

God tells Moses to go back to Egypt where he was born and rescue God's people, the Israelites, from their slavery. Moses offers multiple excuses to God. The first seems reasonable: The Israelites won't believe that God appeared to Moses. God gives Moses three signs that will signal to the Israelites that divine power was made available to him. Moses' second excuse is a little flimsy. He says he's not the best of speakers. Like the first, God has this excuse covered as well. He offers Aaron, Moses' brother to speak on Moses' behalf. Finally, through the third excuse, comes the real reason for Moses' reluctance. Moses doesn't want this mission from God. He pleads with God to send someone else. (Have a student read out loud the story found in Exodus 4:1-17—or have group members read it quietly to themselves.)

ASK

What excuse do you usually use when you don't do your homework?

DISCUSS, BY THE NUMBERS

1. If Moses was afraid to talk for God, then your group members probably will be the same. Discuss the situations that scare your group members the most. Tell a story about your fears and how God has helped or is helping you overcome this fear.

2. Talk together about how excuses to God are a demonstration of our lack of faith in God's ability to provide what we need.

3. Ask, "Are you more like Moses who initially begged God to give the job to someone else or are you eager to do whatever God wants you to do?"

4. Explore the two questions, "What do you think of Abby's response to God? How often do you think like Abby?"

5. Use this exercise to see how your group members view God. The more patience we attribute to God the closer we are to describing the true character of God. Talk about how we often see God in relationship to what God has done for us. If God has done as we requested then we see God as compassionate and caring. If not, then we often see God as mean and vengeful. Talk about the true nature of God—holy and merciful.

6. Talk together about why we can be so stubborn when it comes to serving Christ. Ask, "How can you let go of your stubbornness and more willingly do what God wants you to do?"

THE CLOSE

Moses made excuses to God in an attempt to get God to choose someone else to rescue the Israelites from their slavery in Egypt. Moses didn't have a proper view of God. He thought God was picking on him. As Moses let go of his stubbornness and surrendered his will to God's, he learns that excuses are unnecessary. Serving God becomes easier the more Moses practices surrender to God. Aren't we like Moses? Aren't we often finding excuses like Moses for why we can't serve God? Aren't we stubborn like Moses, resisting God's will for our lives? Let's drop the excuses, hand over our lives to God, and begin to find peace and purpose in our lives.

Moses Heads to Egypt

Pushing God away

1. The Jewish slaves in Egypt believed the message from God given by Moses. If you believe in Jesus, when do you remember first believing?

 ❑ Recently
 ❑ In the last year or so
 ❑ When I was much younger
 ❑ I haven't put my faith in Jesus yet

2. Pharaoh pushed God out of his life again and again. This is what is called a "hard heart toward God."

 Who do you know who is mad at God?
 Who do you know who doesn't believe in Jesus?
 Who do you know who never thinks about their relationship with God?

3. Moses' walking stick represented the power of God. Do you understand how the Holy Spirit gives you the power of God?

 YES   YES   yes   ?   no   NO   NO

4. "Come on," said Jeannie to her friend Allison. "Your mom will never find out. Technically we aren't lying. We just aren't going to see the movie we said we were going to see. My mom doesn't care."
 Allison considered this logic. Yes, she was going to the movies with her friend Jeannie so she wasn't lying about that. It was just that pesky little fact that the movie that Jeannie wanted to see was not something her mom would approve of.
 How bad could it be, thought Allison, *if Jeannie's mother doesn't mind?*
 "Fine," said Allison. "But if my mom says anything when she picks us up just remember to say we saw the other one."

 What do you think of Allison's logic? How will Allison's decision hurt her relationship with Christ?

5. The people of God worshiped the Lord when they saw God's power through the miracles performed by Moses.

 What do you like most about your congregation's worship service?
 What do you like least?

READ OUT LOUD

The Pharaoh who ruled Egypt at the time of Moses was cruel to God's people. He had pushed the God of the Israelites out of his life. Pharaoh wanted nothing to do with the God of the Bible. Pharaoh acted like he was a god. Why would he need the Hebrew God? God always honors our free will. God allowed the Pharaoh to reject him. Pharaoh had so hardened his heart that God kept it hard. It was like God said, "Okay, you want nothing to do with me? I'll remove myself from you." While Pharaoh pushed God away, out of his life, the Israelites believed in God's mercy and promise to rescue them. (Have a student read out loud the story found in Exodus 4:18-23 and 27-31—or have group members read it quietly to themselves.)

ASK

What food can't you push away when it is offered to you?

DISCUSS, BY THE NUMBERS

1. The Pharaoh of Moses' time chose to put his faith in himself and the false gods of Egypt. What we believe is important. Our faith has eternal consequences. Use this time to talk about how and why we put our faith in Jesus.

2. God gave us a free will so that we can willingly choose to accept or reject Jesus. Use this exercise to talk about how some of those we know want a relationship with Christ while others push Christ out of their lives. Take a few minutes to pray for those identified by your group members who are mad at God, who don't believe in Jesus, or who never think about their relationship with God.

3. Use this item as an opportunity to talk about God's resurrection power that is available to every Christian through the Holy Spirit. The third person of the Trinity is not the God we often discuss. Let your group members ask questions about the Trinity and the Holy Spirit. Give the question back to the group to answer. If there is much confusion or questions about the role of the Holy Spirit in our lives, you may want to devote an additional session to this important topic.

4. Together answer the question, "What do you think of Allison and Jeannie's plan for how they'll explain what movie they saw?" Talk about why we too often try to believe the minimum to be a Christian and do the minimum to act like a Christian.

5. Read Exodus 4:29-31 out loud. Here's your opportunity to lead a faith conversation about the importance of worship.

> Moses and Aaron brought together all the elders of the Israelites, and Aaron told them everything the LORD had said to Moses. He also performed the signs before the people, and they believed. And when they heard that the LORD was concerned about them and had seen their misery, they bowed down and worshiped. (Exodus 4:29-31)

THE CLOSE

We are free to choose Jesus or to live our lives on our own terms. God created us with free will. God didn't want us to robotically love or follow him. In today's story the Pharaoh pushed God away. He wanted nothing to do with God. In contrast, the Israelites drew closer to God. They wanted what God had to offer them. The choice is the same today as it was in the days of Moses. Who will you choose?

1. Pharaoh told Aaron and Moses that he didn't know the God they worshiped. Pharaoh didn't care to know the Lord. How many people do you know who don't want to follow Jesus?

- ❑ Nobody I know
- ❑ A few people I know
- ❑ Most people I know
- ❑ All of the people I know

2. The people of God were punished by Pharaoh for wanting to worship the Lord.

If our government refused to let me worship the Lord, I would—

3. Pharaoh worked the Israelite slaves into exhaustion, perhaps hoping that they would be so tired they would forget about God. I would probably forget about God if I were—

- ❑ a star athlete.
- ❑ the wealthiest person in town.
- ❑ living in poverty.
- ❑ suffering with cancer.
- ❑ the most popular person at school.
- ❑ the smartest person in my school district.
- ❑ a famous teen celebrity.

4. When things didn't work out right away for the Israelite slaves, they got mad at Moses. When things don't work out like I want them to I need to—

- ❑ remember that sometimes things get worse before they get better.
- ❑ turn right away to God instead of blaming.
- ❑ pitch a fit.
- ❑ turn the situation over to Jesus.
- ❑ count my blessings.
- ❑ whine and complain.
- ❑ worship the Lord.
- ❑ ask God for insight into what he is trying to teach me.
- ❑ take a breath and patiently wait on the Lord.
- ❑ drink alcohol or smoke marijuana.

5. Danny knew it was for the best. His parents had been fighting for a long time. It got to the point where they didn't care who they fought in front of, even Danny and his little brother. It was definitely quieter now that his dad had moved out but it just felt weird. Danny thought that things might get better if his parents spent some time apart, but now his mom was talking about divorce. Divorce! Things would never be the same. Danny prayed but nothing happened. It didn't seem fair. God didn't care!

Why do you think things often get worse before they get better? How do you hang in there when Jesus feels so far away?

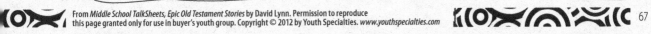

READ OUT LOUD

Moses and Aaron demanded that Pharaoh release the people of God. Pharaoh, who had turned his heart from God, of course answered with a strong "no." And then he made the work of the slaves harsher. The Israelites, God's people, were horrified. How would they keep up with the new demands? The Jewish slave bosses were beaten for not making the slaves produce more. Pharaoh had no fear of the God of the Bible. He saw no need to obey this foreign God. The Pharaoh was the one with the power or so he thought. (Have a student read out loud the story found in Exodus 5:1-23—or have group members read it quietly to themselves.)

ASK

How long do you think you can hang upside down?

DISCUSS, BY THE NUMBERS

1. Read Exodus 5:2 out loud. Lead a faith conversation that explores why some people today, known by your group members, don't want to follow Jesus. Possible reasons: We've not shared the Good News of God's love with them; they don't believe there is a God; they don't see how God has a claim on their life; they don't spend any time thinking about God; they want to live their life their way rather than God's way; they arrogantly believe the truth lies outside the Bible.

> Pharaoh said, "Who is the LORD, that I should obey him and let Israel go? I do not know the LORD and I will not let Israel go." (Exodus 5:2)

2. Listen to the responses to the sentence stem, "If our government refused to let me worship the Lord, I would—." Remind your group members that the world is filled with tyrants who refuse to allow their people the freedom of religion that countries in the West have experienced. Ask, "How should we pray for these people?"

3. Lead a faith conversation into what it takes to get your group members to neglect their relationship with Christ. Ask, "How can we prevent this from happening?"

4. The checked boxes describe appropriate responses to the sentence stem, *When things don't work out like I want them to I need to*—
   - ☑ remember that sometimes things get worse before they get better.
   - ☑ turn right away to God instead of blaming.
   - ☑ pitch a fit.
   - ☑ turn the situation over to Jesus.
   - ☑ count my blessings.
   - ☑ whine and complain.
   - ☑ worship the Lord.
   - ☑ ask God for insight into what he's trying to teach me.
   - ☑ take a breath and patiently wait on the Lord.
   - ☑ drink alcohol or smoke marijuana.

5. Talk together about the answer to the questions, "Why do you think things often get worse before they get better? How do you hang in there when Jesus feels so far away?"

THE CLOSE

We live in a world scarred by sin. In a fallen world filled with evil, things will sometimes get worse before they get better for both believers and unbelievers alike. Things got worse for both the Egyptians and the Israelites and things will sometimes get worse in your life. The miraculous thing about being a follower of Christ is that Jesus doesn't abandon us when the going gets tough. He hangs in there with us, giving us a living hope. Whatever you are facing today will eventually pass—and you can hang in there until it does pass because Jesus is with you!

29. Exodus 7:8-13—Staff into snake;
7:14-25—Water to blood;
8:1-4—Frogs; 8:16-17—Gnats;
8:20-23—Flies; 9:1-4—Dead animals;
9:8-9—Sores; 9:13-16—Hailstones;
10:3-6—Locusts; 10:21-23—Darkness

God Gets Real with Pharaoh

Learning the hard way

1. Pharaoh, the leader of Egypt during the time of Moses, was arrogantly stubborn. Not one to learn from his mistakes, he suffered along with his people, plague after plague. Do you think you learn from your mistakes?

❏ Never ❏ Now and then
❏ Some of the time ❏ Most of the time
❏ All of the time

2. This story of the Plagues is a story of the Pharaoh and God in a battle. Decide if you A (agree) or D (disagree) with these statements about the battles you face.

_____ I don't believe there is a Satan who is fighting a spiritual battle for our souls.
_____ Jesus has already won the battle with Satan.
_____ As a follower of Jesus I often want to follow the ways of the world.
_____ I am not prepared to battle with evil.
_____ Most of my friends are on the evil side of the spiritual battle.

3. Pharaoh refused to obey God. When is it the easiest for you to obey Christ? When is it most difficult?

4. Pharaoh said "no" to placing his faith in God. What did it take for you to put your faith in Jesus?

❏ I just can't believe in this Jesus thing.
❏ I'm close to putting my faith in Jesus.
❏ I used to believe in Jesus but I'm not sure anymore.
❏ I put my trust or faith in Jesus when I was really young. It was easy because I was raised in the church.
❏ I was baptized as an infant so it came naturally to me.
❏ I put my faith in Jesus after struggling with all kinds of questions.
❏ Other: _____

5. "What are you doing?" Julie's father asked.
Julie rolled her eyes; clearly her dad could see she was watching TV.
"Uh, watching TV," Julie said.
"I thought you decided not to watch TV on school nights," her father said. "That was part of your plan to get better grades this semester. Remember?"
Trying not to roll her eyes again, Julie said, "Don't worry Dad. My classes are much easier this semester. I'll be fine."

Is Julie someone who has to learn the hard way? What advice do you think Jesus might give Julie?

READ OUT LOUD

Moses goes again and again to the Pharaoh or King of Egypt, asking that he let go of the people of God. Nine times he goes, followed by nine Plagues from God. But the Pharaoh never learns. His arrogance and stubbornness block his ability to learn the easy way. His refusals come at a great price. (Have a student read out loud the stories from the following various verses in Exodus 7-10—or have group members read them quietly to themselves.)

> Exodus 7:8-13—Staff into snake; 7:14-25—Water to blood; 8:1-4—Frogs; 8:16-17—Gnats; 8:20-23—Flies; 9:1-4—Dead animals; 9:8-9—Sores; 9:13-16—Hailstones; 10:3-6—Locusts; 10:21-23—Darkness

ASK

Which do you think is harder for you to learn—math or a new language?

DISCUSS, BY THE NUMBERS

1. Talk about where and why your group members answered the way they did. Followers of Christ do sometimes act more like Pharaoh (or close to it) than Moses. Use this opportunity to discuss together why we sometimes have to learn the hard way instead of following Christ, who wants what is best for us.

2. See commentary in bold after each statement:
   - I don't believe there is a Satan who is fighting a spiritual battle for our souls. **Some don't believe Satan exists. Remember, disbelief doesn't mean Satan disappears and it certainly doesn't protect you from Satan.**
   - Jesus has already won the battle with Satan. **At the cross Satan was forever defeated but is allowed to continue to discourage believers and distract unbelievers.**
   - As a follower of Jesus I often want to follow the ways of the world. **This conflict is experienced by all followers of Christ. Discuss together how to do spiritual battle with this conflict.**
   - I am not prepared to battle with evil. **Read Ephesians 6:10-18 to get a discussion going about spiritual preparation.**

   - Most of my friends are on the evil side of the spiritual battle. **We want friends who are not believers but we don't want them to be a bad influence on us. We want to be a good influence on them.**

3. Pharaoh refused to obey God. When is it the easiest for you to obey Christ? When is it most difficult?

   Pharaoh suffered through nine plagues. Not until the tenth plague in which he lost his son did Pharaoh acquiesce to God's demand to "let my people go." Ask, "How much suffering and pain are you willing to endure before letting your will go and surrendering it to Jesus?"

4. Use this exercise to talk about what it means to put one's faith in Jesus. Discuss with your group ideas for sharing their faith stories with their friends and relatives.

5. Use this situation to discuss together how your group members can learn from the Bible, from friends, from parents and other adults how to live life without having to suffer the pain of learning the hard way.

THE CLOSE

Pharaoh had to learn the hard way. His stubborn arrogance kept him from submitting his will to the God of the Bible. In contrast to Pharaoh we have Moses who learned to surrender and experience the benefits of following God. Like both Pharaoh and Moses we have a choice, a free will that can resist God's plans for our lives or embrace those plans and follow Christ each new day.

Passover

Faith practices help us experience
God's grace

1. If you were an Israelite slave in the time of Moses, do you think you would have shared your faith in God with the Egyptians you knew?

   ❏ Yes. I think I would have been bold enough.
   ❏ Maybe. I might have had the courage.
   ❏ No. I would have been afraid something bad would have happened to me.

2. God loved his people, the Israelites, so much that he was willing to send plague after plague to force the Pharaoh to release them from slavery.

   I know that God loves me an unimaginable amount because—

3. The false gods in Egypt and the harsh treatment by the Egyptians hindered the Israelites from freely worshiping God. What diverts your attention from the worship of God?

   ❏ Friends
   ❏ Online games
   ❏ Rumors
   ❏ Phone
   ❏ Sports
   ❏ Clothes
   ❏ Homework
   ❏ Chores
   ❏ TV
   ❏ The mirror

4. Since you are free to worship God openly with other Christians, how often do you take advantage of this freedom?

   ❏ Less than once a week
   ❏ Once a week
   ❏ More than once a week

5. Kyle really tried to pray before he went to sleep. He made a mental list of who he knew needed prayer and everything. But every time he tried to do it he started to fall asleep. Then he would wake up, forget where he left off and have to start all over again. This prayer thing was harder than he thought.

READ OUT LOUD

The tenth, last, and most painful plague gets the Pharaoh's attention. This horrific plague of death pushes the Pharaoh to let God's people go. Today's story describes the first Passover, a tradition still practiced by Jews today. Celebrating Passover is a faith practice of the Jews. Christians also have faith practices, those things we do over and over again that keep us close to Jesus. (Have a student read out loud the story found in Exodus 11:1-8 and 12:1-30—or have group members read it quietly to themselves.)

ASK

To get good at a musical instrument or sport how often do you think you need to practice?

DISCUSS, BY THE NUMBERS

1. Read 2 Peter 3:9 out loud. The point of this discussion is to realize that God wants everyone to repent of their sin and be saved. Talk about how the Israelites might have shared their faith in God with the Egyptians. Talk about how we can share our faith with those God has put in our lives. Talk about how sharing our faith is a practice that can strengthen our relationship with Christ.

   The Lord is not slow in keeping his promise, as some understand slowness. Instead he is patient with you, not wanting anyone to perish, but everyone to come to repentance.
   (2 Peter 3:9)

2. Listen to the group members' completed sentences. Use them to lead a faith conversation on the relentless love God has for us. The same love God showered on the Jews as slaves in Egypt, God showers on us. Point out that faith practices are made easier when we experience God's merciful love.

3. Ask, "How can we free ourselves from the distractions that get in the way of our worship of God?" Say something like, "When we let the cares of this world interfere with our worship of God, we are depriving ourselves from experiencing God's presence and power in our lives!"

4. Use this item to talk about the faith practices (or spiritual disciplines) that are observed during worship by your congregation. Here's a list of possible faith practices—
   Prayer
   Bible reading
   Receiving the preaching of God's word
   Giving
   Worship
   Confession
   Observing Communion
   Fellowship
   Silence
   Celebrating
   Evangelizing
   Serving
   Ask, "How do these faith practices draw you closer to Jesus, to experience God's grace?" Discuss together which of these faith practices can be done outside of your congregation's worship service (at home, school, work, sports practice).

5. Use this situation to talk about why faith practices like regular prayer can be so difficult. Ask, "How do we get into a rhythm of doing faith practices? (Hint: How do we do it with piano practice or soccer practice or homework?)

THE CLOSE

The last plague began a ritual that is still meaningful today to Jews around the world. It is a reminder of God's rescue of his people from slavery in Egypt. Jesus is our Passover lamb who rescues us from sin. There are many other faith practices like the Passover that help us experience God's grace on a daily basis—like prayer, Bible reading, confession, evangelism, or service.

Swimming Lessons Unnecessary

God has your back

1. The Israelites turned to God, begging for help when they saw the Egyptian army rushing toward them. When do you usually cry out to God?

   - ❏ Before a math test
   - ❏ When I'm in trouble at school
   - ❏ When I get an A in English
   - ❏ While I'm worshiping with my congregation
   - ❏ When I get grounded
   - ❏ After I break up with a boyfriend/girlfriend
   - ❏ Before I go to bed
   - ❏ Before a big sports event
   - ❏ When I'm really afraid
   - ❏ When my parents are mad at me

   As Pharaoh approached, the Israelites looked up, and there were the Egyptians, marching after them. They were terrified and cried out to the LORD. (Exodus 14:10)

2. After God's people cried out to God to save them from the Egyptian army, they began to grumble about the unfairness of their situation even though God had led them to where they stood. How often do you complain about God's unfairness when God doesn't immediately answer your prayer as you wish?

   - ❏ All of the time
   - ❏ Most of the time
   - ❏ Some of the time
   - ❏ Rarely or never

3. The Israelites feared the evil that could be done to them by the Egyptian army. Circle which of the following gives you the most protection against the evils of this world?

   Boyfriend/girlfriend   Great job   Big bank account   Beer   High school diploma
   Tithing   Serving the poor   Never leaving your house   Other: _____

4. Jennifer usually sat quietly in most of her classes. Her philosophy was not to make eye contact or volunteer and then the teacher would never call on her. But today, the discussion that was taking place in her social studies class moved her to get out of her comfort zone. The topic was world religions and someone in her class said that Jesus was a prophet just like Mohammed. Then someone else said that he was just a really good guy like Buddha. Before she could stop herself, Jennifer was raising her hand. "I believe that Jesus is the Son of God," she said.

   What do you think of what Jennifer did?

5. Since God has your back you will—

   (Check all that apply)
   - ❏ Have an easy life
   - ❏ Always get As even when you don't study
   - ❏ Be forgiven of your sins
   - ❏ Get all the money you want
   - ❏ God will work things out for your good
   - ❏ Never have anything bad happen to you
   - ❏ Never pay any consequences for your sins

READ OUT LOUD

God wanted his people, the Israelites to know that he had their backs. God led them to a place in the desert from which there was no escape. The Pharaoh's army had them trapped. The deep waters of the Red Sea were before them; the army behind, above, and below them. There was no humanly possible escape. They must face the Egyptians and die or drown in the waters of the Red Sea. What was God doing to them? (Have a student read out loud the story found in Exodus 14:1-29—or have group members read it quietly to themselves.)

ASK

Who has your back when you get sick?

DISCUSS, BY THE NUMBER

1. Fear. It was a motivator for the Israelites to beg God for help and it also motivates us to cry to God. Tell a story of when you called on God for help. What motivated your prayer? Was your motivation sincere? Discuss with your group how God led his people, the Israelites, into a place of no escape—a place where they had to depend upon him. God does the same today so that our faith and dependence upon Jesus will be strengthened.

2. Ask, "How was the complaining by the Israelites a lack of trust in God?" "How is your complaining a lack of trust?"

3. Jesus was deliberately left off the list to force your group to think carefully about their answer or answers. They may put "Jesus" or "God" in the "Other" category. There is no guarantee that, as followers of Christ, evil will not affect us. Evil will touch our lives. But a boyfriend/girlfriend, a great job, a big bank account, beer, a high school diploma, tithing, serving the poor, or never leaving your house will not protect us from evil, either. When evil does touch our lives we can be confident that our God has got our backs and any suffering inflicted upon us can be dealt with as Jesus experiences it with us.

4. Like Moses, who confidently told the Israelites that God would rescue them, Jennifer told her class the truth about Jesus. Use this situation to talk about

appropriate and inappropriate ways to confidently tell the truth about Jesus.

5. See commentary in bold after each statement:
   - Have an easy life. **No. But Jesus promised us the Comforter called the Holy Spirit. The Holy Spirit who dwells in every believer is the one who comes along beside us to comfort us and give us hope (See John 14:16, 26).**
   - God will work things out for your good. **Yes. See Romans 8:28.**
   - Always get A grades, even after not studying. **No. Followers of Christ aren't ever promised the easy life. But God will be with you as you study. You can pray for self-control to help you stay disciplined as you study.**
   - Never have anything bad happen to you. **No. Bad stuff happens to everyone, believer or unbeliever, because we live in a fallen, sinful world.**
   - Be forgiven of your sins. **Yes!**
   - Never pay any consequences for your sins. **No. We will pay consequences (see Galatians 6:7).**
   - Get all the money you want. **No but you will have all your needs met.**

THE CLOSE

God has our backs. He is looking out for us so that no matter what happens things will work out for the good. God's purpose for us will not be thwarted. God wants the best for us as we glorify his name and as he molds us to be more like Jesus Christ.

Food from Heaven

The Lord provides for our daily needs

1. Decide which of the following is a need (underline) and which is a want (circle).

Phone   Computer   Shoes   French fries
Car   Pizza   Water   Soda
Dishwasher   Chocolate   TV   Bedroom
Pool   Football   Internet

2. The Israelites, God's people, complained after their rescue from Egypt instead of thanking the Lord and believing in God's promise to care for them.

❑ I am more of a complainer like the Israelites.
❑ I am more of a gratitude person who likes to give thanks to God often.

3. Complete the following three sentence stems:

Complaining like the Israelites is a sin—
I complain when—
I am thankful when—

4. Greed pushed some of the Israelites to take more food than was necessary to meet their daily needs. How greedy are you?

❑ Greedier than most people my age
❑ About as greedy as most people my age
❑ Less greedy than most people my age
❑ Not greedy at all

5. The Israelites didn't have to work for the meat and bread that God provided them. Free food. Woo hoo! Today, Jesus is our free bread from heaven that we didn't deserve or work for. How is Jesus the bread of life for you? For your family?

6. *I really wanted that bike*, thought Will as he kicked his old bike. No one in the neighborhood rode an old bike like this. All his friends would be laughing at him. He told the Lord that when he prayed for the bike. He thought God would care about what he needed. *Guess not*, he thought.

Was Will's request for a new bike a need or a want? What do you think of Will's attitude?

READ OUT LOUD

God led his people into the desert, with its blowing sand, lack of water, and nothing much to eat. Thirty days into their escape, all the food they brought from Egypt was gone. Instead of waiting on God to provide, the people complained about the lack of food. Remember, they had recently seen ten miraculous plagues, watched the Red Sea split open, dry land appear and the Egyptian army defeated. In other words, God had miraculously rescued them from slavery while they did nothing but watch God provide. (Have a student read out loud the story found in Exodus 16:1-20—or have group members read it quietly to themselves.)

ASK

Who prepares most of the meals in your home?

DISCUSS, BY THE NUMBERS

1. God says he will provide food, water, and clothing (see Matthew 6:31-32). These are the basic needs to live. Yet, we often confuse needs and wants. As you look at what your group members underlined (needs) and circled (wants) talk about the perspective of those living in third-world countries. Your group members are blessed to have all of their needs met and many of their wants and yet they still complain just as the Israelites.

2. Read Exodus 16:2-3 out loud. Talk about what it would take to turn your group members from complainers to gratitude people.

   In the desert the whole community grumbled against Moses and Aaron. The Israelites said to them, "If only we had died by the LORD's hand in Egypt! There we sat around pots of meat and ate all the food we wanted, but you have brought us out into this desert to starve this entire assembly to death." (Exodus 16:2-3)

3. Listen to your group members' completed sentences. Discuss how complaining is an option but an option that is ineffective. When we complain we make our circumstances worse. When we complain we take matters into our own hands instead of relying on the Lord and his provision. God knows what is best for us. Let's be thankful and trust in his plan.

4. Greed is a dangerous sin because it compels us to want what is not ours. Stealing, rage, murder and more are all caused by greed. Our selfishness takes our focus off of Jesus and places it on ourselves. When we want to do it our way we get ourselves into trouble. Discuss how your group members can learn to be content with what they have instead of always wanting what others have.

5. Read John 6:48-51. This is a tough question for your group members. Tell a story of how Jesus has been bread from heaven for you—sustenance in a desert like manna was for the Israelites. Ask your group members to share how they think Jesus' death and resurrection not only gives them eternal life but also can sustain them today.

   "I am the bread of life. Your ancestors ate the manna in the wilderness, yet they died. But here is the bread that comes down from heaven, which anyone may eat and not die. I am the living bread that came down from heaven. Whoever eats this bread will live forever. This bread is my flesh, which I will give for the life of the world." (Jesus in John 6:48-51)

6. Use this situation to talk about God's provision and our prayers. Ask, "Is it appropriate to ask God for a new bike like Will did?" When we pray, we are to pray for those things that are within God's will rather than our will. Was Will's prayer request within God's will?" Listen to all opinions without putting any down. This is a tough situation with no quick answer. It will be the discussion about God's will and prayer that is more valuable than coming up with the right answer.

THE CLOSE

The Lord provides for our daily basic needs just as he did for the Israelites in the Old Testament. However, we have expanded "basic needs" of food, water, and clothing to include online games, phones, and the latest fashions. Our greed has created entitlement issues where we think we deserve more and more. This attitude hurts our relationship with Christ because we become so focused on ourselves and the accumulation of more stuff that our priorities become skewed in the direction of the world rather than God.

God Gets Serious on a Mountain

Get serious about your relationship with Jesus

1. When I come to God in prayer I like to—

- ❏ make it short and to the point.
- ❏ check my social networking sites at the same time
- ❏ play music.
- ❏ take a walk.
- ❏ eat a meal to save time.
- ❏ get on my knees.
- ❏ close my eyes.
- ❏ focus on who God is.
- ❏ read the Bible.
- ❏ lower my head.

2. God wanted to get the Israelites to pay attention to him. God spoke through thunder and lightning, fire and smoke, an earthquake, and the blasts of a trumpet. When are you paying the most attention to Jesus?

- ❏ While on a church retreat
- ❏ During Sunday school
- ❏ When I'm alone in my room
- ❏ During a small group Bible study
- ❏ At church camp
- ❏ When I pray before a meal
- ❏ During Communion

3. It was time for the people of God, the Israelites, to get serious about their relationship with God. How about you?

- ❏ I'm really serious about my relationship with Jesus.
- ❏ I'm kind of serious about my relationship with Jesus.
- ❏ I'm not very serious about my relationship with Jesus.
- ❏ I don't have a relationship with Jesus.

4. God's people trembled in the camp after hearing the thunder and trumpet blast and seeing the lightning and thick cloud. What do you think it means to fear God?

- ❏ To be so afraid that you avoid God
- ❏ To have respect for who God is—the creator of the universe
- ❏ To be afraid after every mistake that God will send you to hell
- ❏ To understand that God is an angry, vengeful God

5. Grant's Aunt Jean died. His mom came into his room and told him just now. Grant could tell that she was really sad. Aunt Jean wasn't much older than his mom so it came as quite a shock. She was only sick for like a month. This kind of scared Grant because if it could happen to his aunt, it could happen to his mom or dad, too. He never really thought about his parents dying, until now.

Grant walked out of his room and into the kitchen. His mom hung up the phone. Grant could see that she had been crying.

"I'm sorry about Aunt Jean," he said.

"I know Grant," said his mom as she hugged him. "It just came as such a surprise. I'm just so glad that she is with Jesus and we will see her again."

Grant hugged his mom back. He still was upset but didn't feel as bad as he did before.

Why do you think it is important for Grant to have an intentional relationship with Jesus?

READ OUT LOUD

God's people, the Israelites, have been rescued by God out of slavery in Egypt. They miraculously crossed the Red Sea and received food from God. Now, two months out of Egypt, they are camped in the desert at the foot of Mt. Sinai. Moses goes up the mountain where God gives him a message to give to the Israelites. God's people are to remember the miracles they have experienced, to faithfully obey God and to get serious with their relationship with God. Moses leads the people out of their camp to meet the Lord. (Have a student read out loud the story found in Exodus 19:16-25—or have group members read it quietly to themselves.)

ASK

In what class do you need to get more serious?

DISCUSS, BY THE NUMBERS

1. Ask your group members to decide which of the responses respect God's holiness and status as God and which don't. Your group can also add other ideas. The point is to have a faith conversation on how we can show our reverence and respect for God. This is something that the Israelites learned in today's story.
   - make it short and to the point
   - get on my knees
   - check my social networking sites at the same time
   - close my eyes
   - play music
   - focus on who God is
   - take a walk
   - read the Bible
   - eat a meal to save time
   - lower my head
2. Ask, "How do these times help you pay attention to Jesus?" Today's story illustrates that God wants us to pay attention to our relationship with him. We can choose to neglect that relationship or pay attention to it.
3. Ask for examples of how your group members see themselves getting serious with Jesus. Give a story or two from your life about the seriousness of your relationship with Christ. Talk about the importance of being intentional about your relationship with Jesus.
4. Read Exodus 19:16 out loud. The correct answer is the second one. However, the other three choices are too often common thinking. Somehow God is to be avoided or feared because he is a punisher of sin and a vengeful God who wants to harm us. You can dispel this myth by talking about God's merciful grace.
5. Get a faith conversation going about the importance of growing your relationship with Christ now, while life is going well, so that when the hard times come you can confidently and intentionally know how to rely on Jesus.

THE CLOSE

The Israelites' stay at the foot of Mt. Sinai was a special time in which God called his people to get serious about their relationship with him. They learned that God was unique, different than the gods of Egypt. God was a holy and powerful God who must be treated with respect and reverence. God was also a loving and merciful God who provided for all their needs. That same God is the God we serve today.

The Ten Commandments

God's rules are for our protection

1. Make God number one.
2. Worship God alone.
3. Honor God's name.
4. Rest one day a week to renew yourself spiritually.
5. Obey your parents and grandparents.
6. Do not murder.
7. Keep sex in marriage.
8. Don't steal.
9. Don't lie.
10. Don't be envious of what others own.

1. How many of the Ten Commandments do you think your friends could name?

❏ All 10   ❏ At least six or seven   ❏ Four or five   ❏ At least three   ❏ None of them

2. How many of the Ten Commandments are broken in the average video game?

❏ All of them   ❏ Most of them   ❏ Some of them   ❏ None of them

3. Which of the Ten Commandments do you think is kept the most?

4. What do the Ten Commandments teach about God?

❏ God is no fun.
❏ God is loving.
❏ God knows that people need boundaries.
❏ God enjoys watching people struggle to keep the Ten Commandments.

❏ God wants a personal relationship with us.
❏ God knows that people are broken.
❏ God is a God of mercy which is why he gave these commandments in the first place— to help us live life in a relationship with him.

5. Alison sat on the overstuffed chair in the living room. Normally this was a really comfortable chair to relax on but not today. Today she was sitting there, waiting for her mother and father to return to inform her of her fate. Somehow, through their super-parent detection powers probably, they found out that she had been using the computer while they weren't home. This was in violation of a major family rule. Alison decided not to push her luck and lie about it and just told them the truth. Yes, she had been using the computer when they were gone. Alison looked up as her parents entered the room.

"Alison," said her father. "You know that what you did was wrong. But we do appreciate that you told us the truth about it. That at least shows that you respect yourself and our family enough not to lie. If you had lied, the consequence would have been much harsher."

How do you think the family rule about the computer protects Alison when she follows it?

6. How do you think the Ten Commandments protect us?

❏ They give us boundaries that, if we stay inside those boundaries, keep us safe from negative consequences.
❏ They don't. They are for Old Testament times.
❏ They remind us that rules are made to be broken.
❏ They let us know that we can do anything we want because God will forgive us.

READ OUT LOUD

Outdated rules that are irrelevant for our 21st-century world; that's the view many people have of the Ten Commandments. Spoken by God from Mt. Sinai while the people stood at the foothills of the mountain, the Ten Commandments were to be taken seriously. After speaking them God wrote them down on two stone tablets and gave them to Moses to take to God's people. God knew his people would stray from the truth and harm themselves in their sins. So the two stone tablets were a reminder to obey the Lord. (Have a student read out loud the Ten Commandments found in Exodus 20:1-21—or have group members read them quietly to themselves.)

ASK

What is your number one family rule?

DISCUSS, BY THE NUMBERS

1. Say something like, "Everyone seems to know about the Ten Commandments but few people can name them all." Ask, "How many of the Ten can you name without looking at the list?"

2. This question makes for an interesting discussion especially since most people continue to play games in spite of their content. Remember to listen to all opinions without put-downs.

3. Explore why they think this particular one of the Ten is kept the most. Ask, "Why would people keep this one and not the others?" Often, young people will say Commandment #6, "Do not murder" because it affects others. Talk together about how all ten affect more than just you. Any commandment that is broken affects others.

4. The statements that are checked are examples of what the Ten Commandments teach.
   - ☐ God is no fun.
   - ☑ God is a loving God.
   - ☑ God knows that people need boundaries.
   - ☐ God enjoys watching people struggle to keep the Ten Commandments.
   - ☑ God wants a personal relationship with us.
   - ☑ God knows that people are broken.
   - ☑ God is a God of mercy which is why he gave these commandments in the first place—to help us live life in a relationship with him.

5. Use this situation to talk about the consequences for not keeping the Ten Commandments. Consequences are not from God but from society because without consequences we would live in chaos. Say something like, "We often see consequences as a bad thing yet, without them our society would fall apart." The consequences of not following the Ten Commandments are both personal (like what happened to Alison) and communal (effects on society).

6. The answer to "How do you think the Ten Commandments protect us?" is the first choice: boundaries.

THE CLOSE

God gave his people in the Old Testament ten simple rules to follow so that their lives would be better. God knew that we need boundaries to help keep us on track. Without boundaries we will do anything we want which can only harm us. Many people think that the Ten Commandments are old fashioned and don't apply in our 21st-century world. Yet, when you actually study them you find that they are relevant for today—that they help a society function in an orderly fashion where everyone can get along.

More Rules to Live By

Act justly, love mercy

1. God hates the spreading of rumors or any other kind of evil talk.

Have you been injured by someone else's evil talk?
❑ Yes   ❑ No
Have you directed evil talk at others?
❑ Yes   ❑ No

"Do not spread false reports. Do not help a guilty person by being a malicious witness." (Exodus 23:1)

2. Which one is easier?

❑ Follow the crowd in doing wrong.
❑ Resist the crowd and do what's right.

"Do not follow the crowd in doing wrong. When you give testimony in a lawsuit, do not pervert justice by siding with the crowd." (Exodus 23:2)

3. God demanded way too much when he asked his followers to love their enemies.

❑ I strongly agree   ❑ I agree   ❑ I disagree   ❑ I strongly disagree

"If you see the donkey of someone who hates you fallen down under its load, do not leave it there; be sure you help them with it." (Exodus 23:5)

4. What do you think?

	DEFINITELY	SOMETIMES	NOPE
a) The poor simply need to work harder.	❑	❑	❑
b) Our church should help the poor.	❑	❑	❑
c) The poor never get a fair trial.	❑	❑	❑
d) God doesn't expect his followers to help the poor.	❑	❑	❑
e) Poor people don't change.	❑	❑	❑

"Do not deny justice to your poor people in their lawsuits." (Exodus 23:6)

5. Today's Bible passage (Exodus 23:9) is referring to illegal immigrants.

❑ I strongly agree   ❑ I agree   ❑ I disagree   ❑ I strongly disagree

"Do not oppress a foreigner; you yourselves know how it feels to be foreigners, because you were foreigners in Egypt." (Exodus 23:9)

READ OUT LOUD

God wanted his people to treat each other fairly and get along with each other. After the Ten Commandments, God handed out a few more rules to help his people. (Have a student read out loud some of them from Exodus 23:1-9—or have group members read them quietly to themselves.)

ASK

How do rules make games fair?

DISCUSS, BY THE NUMBERS

1. Read Exodus 23:1 out loud. Tell a story of how you have been hurt by evil talk as well as how you have hurt others. After answering the questions, talk together about how God's rules were designed to protect us.

> *"Do not spread false reports. Do not help a guilty person by being a malicious witness."*
> *(Exodus 23:1)*

2. Read Exodus 23:2. Both young people and adults follow the crowd. When young people do it, it's called "peer pressure"; when adults do it, it's called "office politics." Sometimes it is easier to do what is right rather than follow the crowd. Too often, however, it is easier to be a crowd-follower. Lead a faith conversation on crowd-following when it leads us to do wrong. Ask, "Why is crowd-following to do wrong such a common practice?"

> *"Do not follow the crowd in doing wrong. When you give testimony in a lawsuit, do not pervert justice by siding with the crowd."*
> *(Exodus 23:2)*

3. Read Exodus 23:5 out loud. See what Jesus says in Luke 6:27-36.

> *"If you see the donkey of someone who hates you fallen down under its load, do not leave it there; be sure you help them with it." (Exodus 23:5)*

4. Read Exodus 23:6 out loud. Use the verse as a guide as you lead a faith conversation on the poor. Ask, "How did Jesus treat the poor?"

> *"Do not deny justice to your poor people in their lawsuits." (Exodus 23:6)*

5. This is a controversial issue that is heated on all sides yet unfortunately many Christians don't look at what the Bible has to say. Read Exodus 23:9 out loud to help guide your discussion.

> *"Do not oppress a foreigner; you yourselves know how it feels to be foreigners, because you were foreigners in Egypt." (Exodus 23:9)*

THE CLOSE

The people of God needed the Ten Commandments as well as other basic rules to help guide their actions both individually and collectively. Today's Bible passage gave us some of those basic rules as well. Many of our laws today are based on English common law which used the laws of the Old Testament as their basis. God summarized these rules in Micah 6:8: *He has shown you, O mortal, what is good. And what does the LORD require of you? To act justly and to love mercy and to walk humbly with your God.*

The Israelites Test Another Path to God

All roads don't lead to God

1. How are you like the Israelites who built their own god to worship?

- ❏ It's easy for me to think that sports are everything.
- ❏ I get distracted by my friends, music, the mall, and start thinking I'm really cool.
- ❏ I forget about Jesus because I've got homework which is really important to me.
- ❏ My computer games divert my attention from God to beating my friends.
- ❏ My friends who believe in other religions tempt me to convert.

2. God's people were ready to go back to Egypt. They built the golden calf god to guide them back. Why do you think they wanted to go back to slavery in Egypt?

- ❏ They were afraid of the unknown.
- ❏ They enjoyed being slaves.
- ❏ They didn't like to worship God.
- ❏ They thought they made a mistake leaving Egypt.
- ❏ They were tired of walking in the desert.
- ❏ They were tired of vacationing with Moses and wanted to get back to work.
- ❏ They had no clue what they wanted.

3. How many weeks away from your congregation does it take for you to start forgetting about Jesus?

❏ A week   ❏ Less than a month   ❏ A month or two   ❏ More than two months

4. The Israelites took the wealth that God gave them and worshiped it. How do we worship our money and stuff today? Why is this a sin? Why do you think we do this? How can we avoid this?

5. "But really," said one of the guys in Marcus' history class. "Doesn't every religion talk about God in some form?"

"Yes," said Mrs. Parker. "All religions offer a pathway to what we call God."

Oh, brother, thought Marcus. I can't believe I have to sit here and listen to this junk. Yesterday we talked about a religion that thought cattle were gods. Another religion that we had to read about said that we would just keep coming back as different things until we got it right and could get to heaven. Why is it so hard for these people to just believe in the God that the Bible talks about?

What do you think of Marcus' attitude? Is Mrs. Parker correct? What should Marcus do?

READ OUT LOUD

Moses had gone up Mt. Sinai to receive the Ten Commandments written by God on two stone tablets. While he was meeting with God, the people of God decided that they needed a new god to lead them, believe it or not, back to Egypt. Since Moses had not yet come back from Mt. Sinai perhaps the Israelites thought their God had abandoned them. They had not yet realized that their God was the one and only true God. For them any god would do. (Have a student read out loud the story found in Exodus 32:1-8—or have group members read it quietly to themselves.)

ASK

How many different religions can you name?

DISCUSS, BY THE NUMBERS

1. As humans we are capable of worshiping anything that moves or doesn't move when we reject worship of the Triune God. Say something like, "Many people believe that all religions lead to God and heaven." Lead a faith conversation about the fact that God did create us to worship him. We have been created to be friends with God. When people reject Jesus they fill the void with other religions or things to worship. See commentary in bold after each statement.

   - It's easy for me to think that sports are everything. **Sports are great until they become more important than God. That's when we begin to worship the sports "idol."**
   - I get distracted by my friends, music, the mall, and start thinking I'm really cool. **We can worship ourselves when our "coolness" becomes more important than God.**
   - I forget about Jesus because I've got homework which is really important to me. **Our studies, our preparation for college or career are critical until they replace God. That's when our priorities are skewed and we need to again put God first.**
   - My computer games divert my attention from God to beating my friends. **It's easy to worship our games instead of our God.**
   - My friends who believe in other religions tempt me to convert. **When we begin to think that all religions are the same we become deceived.**

2. Use this exercise to talk with your group about why we as Christians sometimes want to go back to sin instead of the freedom we have in Christ.

3. Lead a faith conversation about how easy it can be to turn away from Christ. Tell a story about your friends who have turned away and what you do to ensure that you stayed grounded in Jesus.

4. The Israelites took their wealth, given to them by God (see Exodus 12:35-36) and literally worshiped it instead of giving the glory to God. Discuss together how we take God's blessings like our good looks, athletic ability, intelligence, artistic talent, or money and use them for sinful purposes.

5. Use this situation to talk about what our reaction should be toward other religions. How can we respect others' beliefs without compromising our own beliefs?

THE CLOSE

Jesus clearly says, "*I am the way and the truth and the life. No one comes to the Father except through me.*" (John 14:6) There's only one way to have a relationship with God, and that's through putting our faith in Jesus.

Rebellion in the Desert

God is merciful, even when we rebel

1. How have you seen people rebel against God?

- ❏ Sin boldly, not caring how it hurts God.
- ❏ Say there is no God.
- ❏ Think only of self.
- ❏ Try to hide their sins from God.
- ❏ Other: _____

"Only do not rebel against the LORD. And do not be afraid of the people of the land, because we will devour them. Their protection is gone, but the LORD is with us. Do not be afraid of them." (Numbers 14:9)

2. How do you think people treat God with contempt?

- ❏ Ignore Jesus.
- ❏ Make fun of Jesus.
- ❏ Pretend there is no God.
- ❏ Make fun of people who believe in Jesus.
- ❏ Disrespect God's name.

The LORD said to Moses, "How long will these people treat me with contempt? How long will they refuse to believe in me, in spite of all the signs I have performed among them?" (Numbers 14:11)

3. What is the first thing you thought of when Numbers 14:18 was read today? Do you believe it? Why or why not?

"The LORD is slow to anger, abounding in love and forgiving sin and rebellion." (Numbers 14:18a)

4. The Israelites paid consequences for their sins even though God had forgiven them. Forgiveness does not mean the consequences of our sins disappear. Do you usually think of the consequences before you sin?

- ❏ Every time
- ❏ Most of the time
- ❏ Some of the time
- ❏ Hardly ever or never

5. For as long as Chad could remember all he knew was church, church, church! His family went to church on Sunday, church parties, Bible studies, and on and on and on. When he was a little kid it was no big deal because he really didn't know anything else. But now his friends were going on overnighters and camping trips that would keep him from church on Sundays. He had gone a couple of times and really enjoyed it. Okay, so they swore a lot and told some questionable jokes but that was a "guy thing," right? Chad was starting to realize what he had been missing. It was time to do other things besides go to church. One of the guys invited him over to play the new video game that his parents wouldn't even let him see the previews for. It was going to be great!

What do you think of Chad's decision?

READ OUT LOUD

God's people send out 12 spies to check out the Promised Land. Ten come back with a report of gloom and doom. Two, Joshua and Caleb return with a message of hope and victory. The people want nothing to do with the hopeful message, listening instead to the majority report. They rebel, telling Moses again that they want to go back to slavery in Egypt. The Lord is furious with his people for not trusting in him. Yet, his mercy and compassion lead him to forgive them. (Have a student read out loud the story found in Numbers 14:1-25—or have group members read it quietly to themselves.)

ASK

Who shows you mercy no matter what you do?

DISCUSS, BY THE NUMBERS

1. Read Numbers 14:9 out loud. Let your group members share stories of how they have seen people rebel against God.

    "Only do not rebel against the LORD. And do not be afraid of the people of the land, because we will devour them. Their protection is gone, but the LORD is with us. Do not be afraid of them." (Numbers 14:9)

2. In spite of the signs God has given the people of this world through the design and wonder of creation, people continue to treat God with contempt. Lead a faith conversation on the ways people do this (ignore Jesus, make fun of Christ, pretend there is no God, disrespect God's name, make fun of people who believe in Jesus).

    The LORD said to Moses, "How long will these people treat me with contempt? How long will they refuse to believe in me, in spite of all the signs I have performed among them?" (Numbers 14:11)

3. Read Numbers 14:18a. Discuss together how the God of the Old Testament is the same God in the New Testament. People often think that the Old Testament God is an angry, vengeful God who pours out his rage on people. The New Testament God is slow to anger and filled with forgiving compassion. The reality is the God of the Old Testament is the same as the New and did pour out his grace on the people living in the Old Testament. Those people who rejected him committed horrible sins that demanded punishment because of God's holiness. God's people, the Israelites, were held to a high standard in the Old Testament because they were to live in such a way as to draw the rest of the world to God. When they disobeyed they were punished because of this higher calling. But God was merciful and loving as today's Bible verse shows.

    "The LORD is slow to anger, abounding in love and forgiving sin and rebellion." (Numbers 14:18a)

4. The Israelites were forced to wander in the desert for 40 years because of their rebellion. The rebellious adult generation had to die before God let their children into the Promised Land of Palestine. We know that God is a merciful and forgiving God but there are consequences for our sins. Fortunately, because Jesus took our sins upon him and paid the eternal consequences, we have been rescued from paying the eternal price ourselves. But we still often pay earthly consequences. Use this question to talk together about those earthly consequences.

5. Use these additional questions to help you discuss this situation: What will be the positive consequences of his decision? What will be the negative? Do you think the positive consequences will outweigh the negative? Why or why not?

THE CLOSE

It's a good thing we don't get what we deserve! If so, we would all be in trouble because we all have rebelled against God. Beginning with Adam and Eve we thought we could live our lives better on our own than with God. And what a mess we have created. Fortunately God is a merciful God who treats us better than we deserve.

You are merciful, and you treat people better than they deserve. So please forgive these people, just as you have forgiven them ever since they left Egypt. (Numbers 14:19 CEV)

You were saved by faith in God, who treats us much better than we deserve. This is God's gift to you, and not anything you have done on your own. (Ephesians 2:8 CEV)

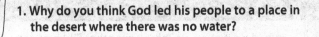

Water from God . . . or from Moses?

Let's be completely confident in God (and God's way of doing things!)

1. Why do you think God led his people to a place in the desert where there was no water?

- ❏ God is really mean.
- ❏ God likes to see people sweat.
- ❏ God wanted his people to trust that he would provide.
- ❏ God forgot that his people needed water to live.

Now there was no water for the community, and the people gathered in opposition to Moses and Aaron. (Numbers 20:2)

2. God provided for the Israelites in the desert, yet they continued to complain. When I look back at what God has done in my life I realize that—

- ❏ God hasn't done much in my life.
- ❏ God has done some things in my life.
- ❏ God has done great things in my life.

"Why did you bring us up out of Egypt to this terrible place? It has no grain or figs, grapevines or pomegranates. And there is no water to drink!" (Numbers 20:5)

3. Moses and Aaron, in their frustration, took charge of getting the water their way instead of God's.

Have you ever done things your way instead of God's way?	Yes No
Have you ever noticed others doing it their way instead of God's way?	Yes No
Have you read other Bible stories about people doing it their way instead of God's way?	Yes No

4. I rely totally on God because I am completely confident in God and his way of doing things.

YES   YES   yes   ?   no   NO   NO

5. Kyle wanted a new bike so badly that he even dreamed about it. He needed one really. His old one was still okay to ride but it looked like a little kid's bike. He prayed and asked God to please make his parents decide to buy him one. He would never admit it but he even showed God a picture during one of his prayers, just to make sure he got the right one. Now he just had to wait. But maybe he should show his parents the picture one more time and tell them about how the guys always make fun of him just so they will know how really important this bike is to him.

Do you think Kyle was confident in God's ability to guide his life or do you think he took matters into his own hands?

READ OUT LOUD

The Israelites were led by God to a place in the desert where Moses and Aaron's sister, Miriam, died. Even though the two brothers were grieving the loss of their sister, the people came before them and complained that they had no water. God told Moses to speak to a rock and water would flow abundantly. An angry Moses hit the rock twice with his staff instead of speaking to it. While we can understand Moses' anger at the complaining people, he had taken matters into his own hands instead of following God's instructions. (Have a student read out loud the story found in Numbers 20:1-13—or have group members read it quietly to themselves.)

ASK

When are you most likely to disobey God even though you know better?

DISCUSS, BY THE NUMBERS

1. Read Numbers 20:2 out loud. The answer is the third choice. God didn't lead his people into the desert for them to complain but for them to learn to trust in his provision. Ask, "Why do you think trusting in Jesus is such a difficult lesson for us to learn?"

   Now there was no water for the community, and the people gathered in opposition to Moses and Aaron. (Numbers 20:2)

2. Read Numbers 20:5 out loud. Talk about times God has provided for you in the past even when it looked bleak. Your group members (and perhaps you as a leader) haven't had as many experiences as older Christians so credible stories of God's provision help your group members see that God can be trusted.

   "Why did you bring us up out of Egypt to this terrible place? It has no grain or figs, grapevines or pomegranates. And there is no water to drink!" (Numbers 20:5)

3. We take things into our own hands when we do things like worry, give up, complain, blame others, don't ask God what he wants us to do. God's way of doing things is always the best and yet we often are impatient. We can't wait for God. So we rush in and do it our way. Talk about other Bible stories where people did it their way instead of God's way. Ask, "What can we learn from these situations?" Also look at what we can learn from our own mistakes and the mistakes of others.

4. Use this statement, "I rely totally on God because I am completely confident in God and his way of doing things" to lead a faith conversation on being completely confident in the Lord. Here are some statements that describe what it looks like to be completely confident in God and his way of doing things. 1) It looks like giving my worries to God; 2) It looks like asking for forgiveness knowing that God will forgive; 3) It looks like relying on what God says in the Bible rather than my own wisdom; 4) It looks like accepting God's answers to prayer as the best instead of hoping I get what I want; 5) It looks like walking by faith instead of by sight.

5. This situation helps your group members get practical with what it means to rely on God. Together answer the question, "Do you think Kyle was confident in God's ability to guide his life or do you think he took matters into his own hands? Ask additional questions like: Was Kyle relying on God or wishing that he would get his way? Who could Kyle talk with about his situation to see what it means to rely on God? How might Kyle know how God answered his prayers? Is having a backup plan the same thing as relying on God?

THE CLOSE

God knows what is best for you just as he knew what was best for Moses, Aaron, and his people, the Israelites. We can be completely confident in God and his way of doing things because the Bible has reliably shown us how God has acted in the past. We can also talk with older Christians to see how they have been able to rely on God. Let's commit to each other to see what our lives would be like if we totally lean on Jesus.

Lousy Food and Not Enough to Drink

God wants our obedience

1. **The Israelites were impatient. They were never content with what God gave them. Do you usually get what you want when you are impatient?**

   ❑ Every time
   ❑ Sometimes
   ❑ It usually makes things worse for me

   But the people grew impatient on the way. (Numbers 21:4b)

2. **When I complain, I am telling God that I don't like how he is working in my life.**

   ❑ I agree   ❑ I disagree   ❑ I don't know

3. **What do you think? Y (yes), N (no) or MS (maybe so)**

   _____ If I don't complain, how will people know that I'm not happy?
   _____ I'll probably never stop complaining.
   _____ I want to stop complaining but don't know how.
   _____ When I have enough money, I'll stop complaining.
   _____ I never complain.

4. **The Israelites' were saved if they looked at the pole with the snake attached. Those who refused to look died. What do you think you would have done?**

   ❑ Swallowed my pride and looked at the pole so I could live.
   ❑ Refused to look at the pole and figured out myself how to get rid of the snake poison in my body.

   The LORD said to Moses, "Make a snake and put it up on a pole; anyone who is bitten can look at it and live." So Moses made a bronze snake and put it up on a pole. Then when anyone was bitten by a snake and looked at the bronze snake, they lived. (Numbers 21:8-9)

5. *Rules. Sometimes it seems like that is all life is about*, **thought Erica. Her teachers had rules she had to obey, her parents had rules, there were rules that she learned about in church. All people seemed to want kids to do was obey the rules.**

   "I'll be glad when I grow up and don't have to worry about rules anymore," Erica muttered to herself.

   Is Erica right or wrong about her no-rules future?

READ OUT LOUD

The people of God were discouraged since they were forced to take a detour. God seemed to have abandoned them. Stuck in the desert with the same food day after day and little or no water, they became impatient. And like always they complained about Moses and God. They never seemed to learn to want to obey God. (Have a student read out loud the story found in Numbers 21:4-9—or have group members read it quietly to themselves.)

ASK

What food could you eat for days and days and never complain?

DISCUSS, BY THE NUMBERS

1. *Contentment* is a word you don't hear much today. Lead a faith conversation on the benefits of contentment with what Jesus has done for us and given to us. Read aloud 1 Timothy 6:6 as the theme verse for your discussion:

   But godliness with contentment is great gain.

2. Complaining is the natural, sinful response to a situation we don't like. It's taking the situation into our own hands instead of relying on God to take care of things. While it may feel good for the moment, it tends to lead to more complaining, making your situation worse.

3. See commentary in bold after each statement:
   - If I don't complain, how will people know that I'm not happy? **Perhaps we should let God be in charge of our happiness instead of trying to manipulate others with our complaining.**
   - I'll probably never stop complaining. **Many people choose this as a strategy for lifelong unhappiness.**
   - I want to stop complaining but don't know how. **Talk together about how to focus on gratitude.**
   - When I have enough money, I'll stop complaining. **It's a myth that wealth will make you happy. In fact, some of the biggest complainers are people who have money but don't think they have enough. You will never have enough money.**
   - I never complain. **Unfortunately, we all complain just like the Israelites. However, with the Holy Spirit's help we can turn our complaining over to Jesus and practice gratitude.**

4. God saved only those who were willing to look at the pole. The brass snake attached to the pole represented the punishment of their sin—the complaining. To look at that brass snake was to admit or confess their sin and to ask by faith for forgiveness. Those who refused to look also refused to acknowledge their sin. To repent of our sins and turn our lives over to Christ means we must swallow our pride and admit that we can't live life on our own terms.

5. Use this situation as an opportunity to talk about the obedience that God wants from us rather than our complaining.

THE CLOSE

God so wanted his people, the Israelites, to want to obey him. Miracle after miracle and rescue after rescue didn't seem to turn their complaining into joy and obedience. What would have happened if they could have seen how much God loved them and cared for them and simply obeyed him? What would happen to us if we learned this lesson?

Israel Gets a New Leader

Is God calling you to shepherd others?

1. Do you see yourself as a leader or a follower?

☐ I am a leader.   ☐ I am a follower.

2. What do you think? Y (yes) or N (no)

_____ I want to be a leader so that I can have a positive influence on others.
_____ Being a leader is really easy.
_____ Our congregation needs more young leaders.
_____ I'm too lazy to be a good leader.
_____ God doesn't expect me to lead.

3. From whom are you learning leadership skills?

☐ My family
☐ My school
☐ Church leaders
☐ My sports team
☐ I don't think I'm learning anything about leadership

4. Think of all the good leaders you know—at your school, sports team, church, and family. What is the number one characteristic of a good leader?

☐ Obedient to God
☐ Encouraging
☐ Funny
☐ Compassionate
☐ Courageous
☐ Immature
☐ Other: _____

5. Rachel couldn't wait for next Sunday. The pastor of her church wanted to get more young people involved in the worship service and she had been chosen to read the Bible passage before the sermon! Her mom was going to help with her reading because there were some really strange names in it. Rachel wanted to be able to read the passage without any mistakes. Maybe if she did it really well more kids would be asked to help out in worship.

How realistic is this situation?

6. I am ready to lead others to Jesus.

YES   YES   yes   ?   no   NO   NO

READ OUT LOUD

Joshua was called by God to lead the Israelites after the death of Moses. God promised that his powerful help will be with the nation as long as it follows the law of Moses. As a member of the church, the body of Christ, every Christian is a leader called by God to perform special tasks. Not everyone is called to be a pastor or a missionary but everyone is called to be a witness to the love and forgiveness of Jesus Christ! Joshua said yes to God's call. (Have a student read out loud the story found in Joshua 1:1-11—or have group members read it quietly to themselves.)

ASK

What do you want to be in charge of when you are an adult?

DISCUSS, BY THE NUMBERS

1. Depending upon the setting and situation your group members will either be leaders or followers. Discuss in which situations your group members are leaders and in which they are followers. For example, in a social studies class they may be followers while at soccer practice they are leaders.
2. Lead a faith conversation on the importance of Christians leading others in your congregation, in their schools, in their after-school endeavors and in their future careers. Christians can have a significant impact in the world by being effective leaders.
3. Identify together what leadership skills they are learning (e.g., writing, facilitating, motivating others, delegating, organizing, communicating, giving direction). Talk together about how followers of Christ can use these skills to serve others within and outside the church.
4. See what your group members identify as the number one characteristic of a good leader. Without discounting what they think, read Joshua 1:7-9 out loud and ask your group members to call out the characteristics of a great leader.

> "Be strong and very courageous. Be careful to obey all the law my servant Moses gave you; do not turn from it to the right or to the left, that you may be successful wherever you go. Keep this Book of the Law always on your lips; meditate on it day and night, so that you may be careful to do everything written in it. Then you will be prosperous and successful. Have I not commanded you? Be strong and courageous. Do not be afraid; do not be discouraged, for the LORD your God will be with you wherever you go." (God in Joshua 1:7-9)

5. Use this situation to discuss together the need for more youth leadership within your congregation. Identify potential roles your group members could play within your congregation. Discuss together the importance of youth stepping up and taking these roles. Talk about the potential roadblocks they may face from adults (most of them unintentional but still very real).
6. I am ready to lead others to Jesus. This is a leadership role all Christ-followers are called to do. Your particular church may not call it "leading others to Jesus" so use your congregation's wording but do talk about our role in evangelism.

THE CLOSE

Like Joshua you are called to lead. You are called to be a witness for Christ. You are called to do special tasks within your congregation. You are called to love your neighbor. You are called to serve others. Joshua said yes to God's call. What will your response be to Jesus?

Rahab and the Spies

God is seldom early . . . but never late

1. God worked through Rahab even though she had made some bad decisions. God can work through me even though I have made some bad decisions!

   ☐ For sure
   ☐ Sometimes
   ☐ Not really

2. Rahab heard of all that God had done for his people, the Israelites—the rescue from slavery in Egypt, the miraculous crossing of the Red Sea, the manna and quail from heaven.

   What is your God story—what has Jesus done in your life?

3. God liked it that Rahab lied.

   ☐ I agree
   ☐ I disagree
   ☐ I'm not sure

4. God went ahead of the two spies to prepare things so that God's will was done. God is working on your behalf in your future even before you get there.

   ☐ I agree   ☐ I disagree   ☐ I have no idea

5. Donny's dad lost his job over a year ago. Since then the family has really cut back; no dinners out, no junk food, and shopping for clothes at resale stores. This was really starting to get old. Donny and his family prayed every night that a job would open up for his father. If it didn't, well, Donny didn't want to think about what could happen. He even heard his mom talking about "losing the house." Then last week, his dad got a job offer. It wasn't as much as he made before but it was a job.

   Do you think the job was a just-in-time God thing? Why or why not? Does life really happen like this?

6. Rahab and her family could have been killed by the Israelites when they invaded Jericho. But God had other plans for them. He saved them just in time. He did the same thing for the two spies. He was there, just in time to help them make their escape. Why do you think God is a just-in-time God?

   ☐ God often forgets about our needs.
   ☐ God has more important things to do than worry about us.
   ☐ God wants us to learn to rely on him instead of ourselves.
   ☐ God gets confused about what needs to happen next.

READ OUT LOUD

You might think that God would condemn and ignore a prostitute. But God saw that she had faith in him. Her and her family's lives were spared. Her faith in God was credited to her as righteousness, just as Abraham's faith. She became the mother* of Boaz and from that lineage came Jesus. Her name made the list of faith heroes**. She was used as an illustration of faith in action***. Just in time, God used Rahab to save the lives of two spies. We learn from this that God is seldom early but never late in acting on our behalf. (Have a student read out loud the story found in Joshua 2:1-24—or have group members read it quietly to themselves.)

*Matthew 1:5
**Hebrews 11:31
***James 2:25

ASK

What is the latest you have ever gotten up in the morning?

DISCUSS, BY THE NUMBERS

1. Read Joshua 2:9b-11 out loud. Use this time to talk about how God works with, in, and through us in spite of our sin. God's grace is there for us when we fall. We repent and keep moving for God. God used Rahab in a big way because she placed her faith in God.

   "I know that the LORD has given you this land and that a great fear of you has fallen on us, so that all who live in this country are melting in fear because of you. We have heard how the LORD dried up the water of the Red Sea for you when you came out of Egypt, and what you did to Sihon and Og, the two kings of the Amorites east of the Jordan, whom you completely destroyed. When we heard of it, our hearts melted in fear and everyone's courage failed because of you, for the LORD your God is God in heaven above and on the earth below."
   (Rahab in Joshua 2:9b-11)

2. This is an opportunity for your group to examine the stories they have about God. Witnessing to others is simply telling our God story—what Jesus has done in our lives.

3. Today's story is not a justification for lying or situational ethics. Rahab took matters into her own hands by lying. Even though her goal was to protect the spies, the end goal never justifies the means by which we meet that goal, which in this case involved lying. Ask, "What could Rahab have done instead of lie?"

4. Many, if not most, of your group members will have never thought about this concept before. Use this as a time to talk about God's omniscience—God's all-knowing presence in our lives. What does it mean to your group members that they serve a God who knows their future and is working for their good even before they arrive at their future?

5. Use this situation to talk about the surprises God gives us as we walk with Jesus. Answer these questions: Do you think the job was a just-in-time God thing? Why or why not? Does life really happen like this?

6. The answer is the third option; God wants us to learn to rely on him instead of ourselves. God is seldom early . . . but never late. God is a just-in-time God so that we will rely on him instead of our own efforts.

THE CLOSE

God accepted Rahab—a prostitute, someone who made some bad choices—because of her faith in God. God turned her life around just in time. We serve a God who is seldom early in helping us . . . but never late!

1. I want Christianity to be easy for me.

YES   YES   yes   ?   no   NO   NO

Crossing the Jordan

The Lord will do powerful things in our lives when we move forward with him

2. God asked the Israelites to cross the Jordan River, a potentially dangerous task. Which *one* of the following dangerous things are you willing to do?

❑ To be ready to suffer for being a follower of Christ (1 Peter 4:16)
❑ To live a life of purity (1 Thessalonians 4:3-8)
❑ To love your enemies (Matthew 5:44)
❑ To care for the hungry, homeless, disenfranchised (Matthew 25:35-36)
❑ To face all kinds of trouble (John 16:33)

3. Do you think that following Christ is a chore or an adventure?

❑ It's a boring chore.
❑ It's an exciting adventure.
❑ Can I get another choice?

4. The Israelites obeyed God by doing a scary thing—walking into the flooded Jordan River. Which of the following scary things would you be willing to do?

❑ I would be willing to live in a Muslim country to be a witness for Jesus.
❑ Talk to five people at my school next week about Jesus.
❑ Sell half of the things I own and give the money to a homeless shelter.
❑ Read my Bible for a week during the time I would spend on my computer.
❑ Pray for one hour a day.

5. Carrie was shocked when she learned that her cousin had cancer. Her mom had just finished talking with Carrie's aunt. Her mom was crying which scared Carrie because her mom hardly ever cried. Carrie didn't know anyone with cancer and to have it happen to someone her own age was really scary. *Okay, God*, thought Carrie. *I really need you big time.*

Could God do something powerful in the life of Carrie's cousin? What might God do?
Could the healing of Carrie's cousin be that God takes her to heaven?

From *Middle School TalkSheets, Epic Old Testament Stories* by David Lynn. Permission to reproduce this page granted only for use in buyer's youth group. Copyright © 2012 by Youth Specialties. www.youthspecialties.com

READ OUT LOUD

God worked a miracle so that his people could walk on dry land across the flooded Jordan River. But the priest and the people had to move forward before the water parted. This was not a safe "religion." Following God required risks. But the Lord did powerful things when the Israelites said, "Yes, we will move forward." (Have a student read out loud the story from Joshua 3:9-17—or have group members read it quietly to themselves.)

ASK

How exciting do you think it will be when you move to high school?

DISCUSS, BY THE NUMBERS

Note to Facilitator: God had parted the waters of the Red Sea 40 years before when the Israelites left Egypt. Now, the Israelites are ready to enter the land God had promised them. To get into the land they must cross the flooded Jordan River. Again, God miraculously parts the water, giving his people a fresh start in a new land.

1. A safe and easy Christianity is not what God has called us to! Explore how ready your group members are to take risks for Jesus. Then talk about what those risks might be—saying yes to loving your enemy and no to bullying; saying yes to positive fun and no to unchaperoned parties; saying yes to small group Bible studies and no to violent video games.

2. Explore each of the actions, why it could be dangerous, and how doing it honors Jesus. Ask different group members to find and read the Bible passages if time permits.
   - To be ready to suffer for being a follower of Christ (1 Peter 4:16)
   - To live a life of purity (1 Thessalonians 4:3-8)
   - To love your enemies (Matthew 5:44)
   - To care for the hungry, homeless, disenfranchised (Matthew 25:35-36)
   - To face all kinds of trouble (John 16:33)

3. For God's people—the Israelites—following God was sometimes a chore; at other times an adventure. In today's story God's people were embarking on an adventure with God.

4. While following Christ is an adventure, it can, at times, be a little scary. Explore why some actions might be scary for your group members to do in the name of Jesus.

5. If we are to follow Christ we must fully surrender our lives to God. Carrie can pray for her cousin then she must leave the results to God. Talk about the powerful things that Jesus will do in our lives if we surrender our will to his will. Perhaps, for Carrie's cousin the most powerful thing Jesus could do to heal her is to take her to heaven!

THE CLOSE

The people of God again walk on dry land through a wall of water to get to the Promised Land. Two miracles, forty years apart, illustrate God's power to work in our lives if we only give our lives over to Jesus. Let us say, "Yes, we will move forward" to God!

The Fall of Jericho

God can tear down the walls in our lives

1. You, like Joshua, have a choice. You can follow God's directions or ignore them. Joshua followed them and the walls of Jericho came crashing down giving God's people a victory.

   When I follow God's directions—
   When I ignore God's directions—

2. Jericho was locked down tight. The walls of the city protected it from intruders. It looked impossible to conquer. Yet, God's people successfully took the city with God's help. What is the first thing you do when you confront the impossible?

   ❑ Run   ❑ Stay focused on the goal and move forward   ❑ Seek help from friends or family
   ❑ Pray   ❑ Struggle along hoping for the best   ❑ Freeze and panic

3. The directions God gave Joshua were very specific. God gave us very specific directions in the Bible. How interested are you in following these directions?

   ❑ Yawn   ❑ Tell me more   ❑ Fascinated

4. Why do you think the God of the Bible wanted all the citizens of Jericho killed?

   ❑ Unlike the God of the New Testament who is loving and merciful, the God of the Old Testament is angry and violent.
   ❑ God didn't want to see them in heaven.
   ❑ God enjoys violence.
   ❑ God had given them more than enough time to repent of their evil ways and could no longer stand their sin.

5. The walled city of Jericho challenged the people of God because it seemed impenetrable. What walls (obstacles or life challenges) do you face?

   ❑ Lack of money   ❑ Bullies   ❑ Rules at school   ❑ Bad grades   ❑ Lack of transportation
   ❑ Young age   ❑ Strict parents   ❑ Rumors about me   ❑ Hurtful friends   ❑ Brothers/Sisters
   ❑ Other: _____

6. *Oh no*, thought Eddie as he looked at his assignment sheet for his reading class. It was Sunday evening, and Eddie decided that he should probably get his work done. He could usually wait this late to do his homework, until this year. He thought he only had to read a book by tonight. But now he realized that he had to read it and do a three-page report on it. There was no way he would get all of that done tonight. When would he learn not to procrastinate?

   How do you think giving his procrastination to Jesus could help Eddie?

From *Middle School TalkSheets, Epic Old Testament Stories* by David Lynn. Permission to reproduce this page granted only for use in buyer's youth group. Copyright © 2012 by Youth Specialties. www.youthspecialties.com

READ OUT LOUD

Jericho was a city filled with the most evil of people. Fearing an imminent attack by the people of God, the citizens of Jericho locked down the city. No one could get in or out. The citizens were secure within their city walls or so they thought. The invasion and destruction of Jericho was ordered by God, not because God is cruel but because his patience had worn thin with the evil of the people of Jericho. (Have a student read out loud the story found in Joshua 6:1-20—or have group members read it quietly to themselves.)

ASK

When you were a little kid would you rather have built a fort or torn it down?

DISCUSS, BY THE NUMBERS

1. Listen to the completed sentences of your group members. Use this time to talk about the consequences of following God's directions as well as ignoring them.

2. Read Joshua 6:2 out loud. God's people were successful against an impenetrable wall because God helped them. Without God they would not have been successful. When we confront the impossible, we, like Joshua, must rely on the Lord to help us. Tell a story of how you faced the impossible with the help of the Lord.

> *"See, I have delivered Jericho into your hands, along with its king and its fighting men." (God to Joshua in Joshua 6:2)*

3. This simple exercise gets at how serious your group members are about following Christ. The following are a few of those specific directions that you can talk about with your group.
   - Don't get drunk. (Ephesians 5:18)
   - Live a life of purity. (1 Timothy 4:12)
   - Obey your parents. (Ephesians 6:2-3)
   - Help the less fortunate in our society. (Matthew 25:35-36)
   - Love God with all you've got. (Deuteronomy 6:5)
   - Tell others of God's love. (Romans 10:14-15)

4. The answer is the fourth choice. Use this statement to begin a faith conversation about God's fairness in commanding the Israelites to wipe out the people living in the Promised Land.

- Genesis 15:13-16 describes how God knew that the people living in the Promised Land would become so sinful that they deserved the punishment they were given by God. They had over four hundred years to repent of their sinful ways yet they chose to continue to become more and more evil.

- Exodus 23:22-33 warns the Israelites not to worship the gods or follow the ways of the people living in the Promised Land of Palestine. God wanted them destroyed because of their evil practices. If they were not driven from the land God knew they would trap God's people in sin (see Exodus 23:33).

- Deuteronomy 9:4-5 tells us that God wanted the people living in the Promised Land wiped out because of their evilness.

5. Lead a discussion about the obstacles or life challenges your group members face. Don't discount what you might see as little walls because they are big in the minds of your group members. Ask, "Are these walls impossible for God to tear down?"

6. Use this situation to talk about a common problem or wall faced by your group members. Ask, "How willing are you to give your procrastination to Jesus?"

THE CLOSE

God did what the people of Jericho believed could never happen. God brought down the walls, destroying their security, and giving God's people the victory. How did this happen? God's people followed God's instructions. We have been given instructions, too. We have the completed Bible—everything we need to know to live for Jesus Christ. So let's keep looking to God's word and asking God for the victory in bringing down the walls in our lives.

God Gives the Israelites a Win

God has a victory strategy for followers of Christ

1. What's the biggest or most fun win you can remember growing up?

- ❏ Great grades
- ❏ Team win
- ❏ Individual competition
- ❏ Board game win
- ❏ Video game
- ❏ Amusement park game
- ❏ I can't remember but I know there was a big one

2. The first attack on Ai ended in defeat because Israel sinned. What does God expect you to do when you sin?

- ❏ I have no idea.
- ❏ Blame someone else.
- ❏ Pretend it never happened.
- ❏ Make lots of excuses.
- ❏ Say "I'm sorry" and change your bad behavior.

3. God reminded Joshua not to get discouraged because of the first defeat at Ai. Why do you think we need a reminder from God to not feel bad about our past mistakes after we have asked God for forgiveness?

- ❏ We still feel guilty.
- ❏ We want God to punish us.
- ❏ We don't feel worthy.
- ❏ We believe we must earn God's forgiveness.
- ❏ We are afraid of God.

4. Joshua won the battle for the town of Ai the second time because he carefully listened to God.

Do you like listening to God through sermons?

YES   YES   yes   ?   no   NO   NO

Do you like listening to God through Bible studies with others?

YES   YES   yes   ?   no   NO   NO

Do you like listening to God through your personal Bible study?

YES   YES   yes   ?   no   NO   NO

Do you like listening to God through prayer?

YES   YES   yes   ?   no   NO   NO

Do you like listening to God through hearing the Bible read?

YES   YES   yes   ?   no   NO   NO

5. They were doing it again. Marissa's friends were gossiping about another girl in their class. The girl looked at them wrong, didn't have the right clothes, or stole someone's boyfriend, pick a reason and they would gossip about someone. This poor girl just didn't "fit." She didn't have the right clothes or haircut so she became the target. Marissa used to join in but lately she felt that maybe this wasn't the way she was supposed to act. She was praying more and reading her Bible and this whole gossip thing just didn't fit in with that.

Why do you think Marissa's strategy of prayer and Bible reading was working?

READ OUT LOUD

After an initial defeat because of Israel's sin, God encouragingly tells Joshua that the Israelites will have a victory over the city of Ai. The Lord gives specific instructions for a winning strategy that, if followed, will lead to success. Joshua enthusiastically follows God's directions and takes the city. (Have a student read out loud the story found in Joshua 8:1-23—or have group members read it quietly to themselves.)

ASK

What board or card game do you often win?

DISCUSS, BY THE NUMBERS

1. Victory celebrations are always fun. They certainly beat losing. Talk about what it means to live victoriously in Christ versus success in the world's eyes. Use examples from your own lives or the lives of people you know personally. Living victoriously in the world's eyes could mean getting drunk and puking on a Friday night. Living victoriously in Christ could mean having an overnighter with friends, having fun without alcohol or other drugs. Living victoriously in the world's eyes could mean texting rumors about someone at school on a Tuesday night. Living victoriously in Christ could mean participating in a small group Bible study with friends on a Tuesday night. Living victoriously in the world's eyes could mean avoiding the loners at school in favor of the "cool" people. Living victoriously in Christ could mean befriending someone who is a loner.

2. Read Joshua 7:11 out loud. Repentance is God's ultimate goal. We need to confess our wrongdoing and change our thoughts and behaviors. Sometimes this process takes years but God is patient and faithful at shaping us to be more like Jesus.

   "Israel has sinned; they have violated my covenant, which I commanded them to keep. They have taken some of the devoted things; they have stolen, they have lied, they have put them with their own possessions."
   (God in Joshua 7:11)

3. Read Joshua 8:1 out loud. Explain the difference between true guilt and psychological guilt. True guilt is what we feel after we have sinned. Psychological guilt is what we feel even after we have asked for forgiveness. It is a guilt caused by not feeling worthy of forgiveness or fear of punishment or abandonment by God. We need to give our psychological guilt to Jesus because we are guaranteed forgiveness.

   Then the LORD said to Joshua, "Do not be afraid; do not be discouraged. Take the whole army with you, and go up and attack Ai. For I have delivered into your hands the king of Ai, his people, his city and his land." (Joshua 8:1)

4. See if there is a favorite that is common among your group. Explore why it is a favorite. Ask, "Who in our congregation other than our pastor is good at listening to God?" "What do you think that person does to listen to God?"

5. Use this situation to consider basic strategies for avoiding potentially sinful situations.

THE CLOSE

God showed Joshua a winning strategy. First, we need to confess our sins and repent when we are wrong. Second, we also need to seek out God's encouragement. We can practice God's presence in our lives by being aware that God is with us. Third, we need to listen to God's instructions. We can do this by being involved in a small group Bible study, by paying attention to the sermon when we worship with our congregation, by taking Communion, and by studying the Bible on our own.

A Fresh Start

God is in the new-beginnings business

1. I am better than the Israelites because I've never worshiped false gods.

- ❑ I strongly agree
- ❑ I agree
- ❑ I disagree
- ❑ I strongly disagree

2. What do you think? Y (yes) or N (no)

_____ Most people I know from school or sports don't worship God.

_____ Most people my age just want to have fun, not think about God.

_____ People today don't talk or think much about sin outside of the church building.

_____ Most people my age don't know what it means to worship.

_____ There are people my age who care a lot more about Jesus than I do.

3. I have publicly professed my faith in God like Joshua asked of the Israelites by—

- ❑ Baptism
- ❑ Taking Communion
- ❑ Talking with someone who is not a believer about Jesus
- ❑ Regular worship with my congregation
- ❑ Telling my faith story (testimony)
- ❑ Church membership
- ❑ Tithing

4. T (true) or F (false)?

_____ If you live in a Muslim country you can freely choose who you will worship.

_____ People can freely choose to go to hell.

_____ You are free to choose to be an atheist (believe there is no God).

_____ God hopes you choose to have a relationship with him.

_____ You must choose to be a Christ-follower if your parents are Christians.

5. "I forgive you," said Matt's mother. Matt let out a huge sigh of relief. He was so worried that his mom would blow up when she saw that he broke one of the figurines that she kept on the coffee table. They were really old. His mom said they were "priceless" because she got them from her grandmother. Now one of them had gotten squashed by Matt's basketball, the basketball that he wasn't supposed to bounce in the house.

Matt didn't waste any time telling his mom. He met her at the door with the pieces when she got home from work. He told her how sorry he was and then stood and waited for his mom to blow. Except she didn't, she put her arms around him and said she forgave him. He felt like a ton of bricks had been lifted off his shoulders.

How is Matt's mother like God? How often does God give us a fresh start, a new beginning?

6. What do people mean when they say, "This is the first day of the rest of your life"? What does God mean by this?

READ OUT LOUD

After all the miracles and all that God has done for the Israelites, there are still some of them that worship the false gods of the people living around them. God's people can't seem to fully commit to God. So Joshua asked for a public commitment—for the people of God to choose who or what they would worship. (Have a student read out loud the story found in Joshua 24:14-25—or have group members read it quietly to themselves.)

ASK

What do you like most about a do-over in sports?

DISCUSS, BY THE NUMBERS

1. Use this to lead a faith conversation on how you and your group members are similar to God's people in the Old Testament. While God asked us to worship him alone because he is the only true God, the Israelites get preoccupied with false gods—gods that can't possibly help them. We are no different in that we try to serve Jesus and money!

2. See commentary in bold after each statement:
   - Most people I know from school or sports don't worship God. **This gives you a picture of where your group members see the culture in which they live. One person may say everyone is a Christian while another says about half of them and they can go to the same school.**
   - Most people my age just want to have fun, not think about God. **Turn this statement around and say, "I just want to have fun, not think about God." Is that you?**
   - People today don't talk or think much about sin outside of the church building. *Sin* **has been almost eliminated from the vocabulary of our secularized culture. This conveniently helps people worry less when they do something wrong.**
   - Most people my age don't know what it means to worship. **In today's story Joshua called the people of God back to true worship rather than worship of false gods. We have to continue to call people to true worship rather than the worship of things, power, and sex.**
   - There are people my age who care a lot more about Jesus than I do. **Use this statement to,**

like Joshua, call your group to a closer relationship with Jesus.

3. Discuss together how a public profession of your faith helps solidify your commitment to Christ. Discuss each of the ways your group members can publicly profess Jesus—baptism, Communion, witnessing, worshiping with others, telling your faith story (testimony), church membership, tithing and any others your group members have done.

4. See commentary in bold after each statement:
   - If you live in a Muslim country you can freely choose who you will worship. **False. It's illegal in most of these countries to convert to another religion.**
   - People can freely choose to go to hell. **True. God doesn't send people to hell. They choose to reject his offer of forgiveness. In effect they choose hell.**
   - You are free to choose to be an atheist (believe there is no God). **True. God will not stop anyone from** *not* **believing in his existence.**
   - God hopes you choose to have a relationship with him. **True. See 2 Peter 3:9.**
   - You must choose to be a Christ-follower if your parents are Christians. **False. If your parents are Christians, you should choose Jesus because you want to follow him.**

5. Use this situation to talk about new beginnings we have because of the person and work of Christ. We are called to forgive because we have been forgiven.

6. Use these questions, "What do people mean when they say, 'This is the first day of the rest of your life'? What does God mean by this?" to explore the fresh starts we get every time we ask God for forgiveness.

THE CLOSE

God is a fresh-start God who is in the business of new beginnings. In today's story Joshua calls the people to recommit to the Lord. This gives them a fresh start with God. We need to recommit ourselves to Jesus. God tells us in 1 John 1:9 that, "If we confess our sins, he is faithful and just and will forgive us our sins and purify us from all unrighteousness." God stands ready to give you a second and third and fourth and . . . chance.

Gideon Gets Picked

God has a special purpose for our lives

1. Gideon was confused. He thought that because he and God's people believed in God, bad things wouldn't happen to them. But bad things were happening. Do you think bad things happen to people who believe in Jesus?

   ❑ No way. If bad things happen to you then you can't be a Christian.
   ❑ Yes. Bad things happen when you don't have enough faith.
   ❑ Yes. Bad things happen to everyone— Christians and non-Christians alike.
   ❑ It has nothing to do with faith or lack of faith.

2. The Lord appeared to Gideon in the form of an angel and spoke with him. God speaks to me through the Bible—

   ❑ only after I eat a spicy meal.
   ❑ I don't read the Bible.
   ❑ just during the Christmas season through Christmas carols.
   ❑ almost every time I read it, listen to it read, or hear a sermon or talk from it.
   ❑ through text messages.

3. Gideon should not have doubted what the Lord had promised to do with his life.

   ❑ That's right. He should have never doubted God.
   ❑ I'm not sure.
   ❑ No. It's okay to question God about what plans he has for us.

4. Gideon objected to God's choice of him as the warrior who would lead Israel. Gideon's faith appeared weak and fragile and unsuited for this special purpose. What do you sense when you consider that God has a special purpose for your life?

   ❑ I don't have faith.
   ❑ That my faith needs strengthening before I'm ready to do anything with God.
   ❑ That my faith is close to being ready to do great things with God.
   ❑ That my faith is ready to do great things with God.

5. God had a special purpose for Gideon's life but not for my life.

   ❑ I absolutely agree.   ❑ I kind of agree.   ❑ I have no idea.
   ❑ I kind of disagree.   ❑ I absolutely disagree.

6. They were playing that commercial again. The one that asks people to give money to help orphan kids overseas. Sarah's parents sometimes give money to the organization but it always seems like there should be more that can be done. The kids look so sad. There must be a way a 13-year-old like Sarah can help.

   ❑ There isn't really much that someone as young as Sarah could do to help.
   ❑ There are a few things that Sarah could do to help.
   ❑ There are many things that Sarah could do to help.

READ OUT LOUD

Gideon lived in an uncertain time in which Israel's enemies, the Amalekites and Midianites raided the land at will, taking what they wanted. Israel had quickly forgotten God and turned to the gods of the peoples living around them, including the Canaanite god, Baal. Israel needed a new leader, one who could lead them back to God, back to safety, and back to prosperity. Gideon—an unlikely choice by human standards—was God' choice. *Discouraged. Defeated. Doubting.* All words used to describe Gideon, yet God shaped him into a leader for the times; a leader mentioned in the "Faith Hall of Fame" of Hebrews 11. Listen to the Lord's leadership call to Gideon. (Have a student read out loud Judges 6:11-24—or have group members read it quietly to themselves.)

ASK

On what kind of secret mission have you always wanted to go on?

- ❑ Space ❑ CIA ❑ Missionary ❑ Military
- ❑ Detective ❑ Science ❑ Foreign Diplomat

DISCUSS, BY THE NUMBERS

1. Read Judges 6:13 out loud. Gideon lived a myth —the false assumption that God keeps believers protected from the evils of this world. Gideon was about to learn a new truth, one that Jesus teaches us in Matthew 5:45b (*He causes his sun to rise on the evil and the good, and sends rain on the righteous and the unrighteous.*). Gideon was hiding out, processing wheat for food, so that hopefully his enemies, the Midianites, couldn't steal it. He would not have thought to pray because he wrongly assumed God had abandoned him. The truth: God is present with us for both the good and the bad.

> *"Pardon me, my lord," Gideon replied, "but if the LORD is with us, why has all this happened to us? Where are all his wonders that our ancestors told us about when they said, 'Did not the LORD bring us up out of Egypt?' But now the LORD has abandoned us and given us into the hand of Midian." (Judges 6:13)*

2. The "angel of the Lord" was most likely Jesus in his pre-incarnate state. Talk about how we can hear God speak to us by reading the Bible, hearing it read and talked about as a sermon.

3. It was easy for Gideon to doubt God's promise of victory over his enemies. How easy is it for us to doubt God's promises? We serve a powerful God who can handle all our doubts. Only a small god would need to punish his followers for doubting. In fact, doubting shows that a person is questioning and searching, something that is normal for adolescents.

4. Read Judges 6:15 out loud. Use this exercise to begin a conversation about how God meets us where we are faith-wise and uses life experiences, prayer, the Bible, and our congregation to help strengthen our faith.

> *"Pardon me, my lord," Gideon replied, "but how can I save Israel? My clan is the weakest in Manasseh, and I am the least in my family." (Judges 6:15)*

5. God had a purpose for a man like Gideon who didn't always live for God and God has a purpose for you and every one of your group members. Explore with your group what their purpose might be. Remind your group that God has given every believer a gift or gifts and wants those gifts to be used to build up the body of Christ.

6. Use this true-to-life situation to take a practical look at the special purpose God has for your group members, especially how they can serve others in the name of Jesus.

THE CLOSE

Young people can't always identify the special purpose that God has for their lives. However, God has given all of us a special purpose—love God with all that we have and love our neighbor (Luke 10:27).

Gideon Trashes an Idol

God wants 100 percent of our worship

1. Gideon was surrounded by people, including his father, who worshiped Baal, a fake god. What types of people are around you?

   ❑ Mostly Christians
   ❑ Mostly non-Christians
   ❑ I'm not sure

2. Which of the following are treated as gods in the United States today?

   ❑ Money   ❑ Science   ❑ Fame   ❑ Pets
   ❑ Cars/Trucks   ❑ Celebrities   ❑ Clothes   ❑ Homes
   ❑ Power   ❑ Phones   ❑ Home Entertainment Centers

3. *Idolatry*=devotion to fake gods that distracts us from knowing and loving Jesus.

   I agree   I disagree   I don't know

4. Missy looked at the new girl sitting by herself at the next table. She always sat by herself. She looked so sad and lonely. The other kids in the cafeteria had at least one other friend to sit with. The new girl had already been at the school for two weeks and still no one wanted to be her friend. Missy thought about sitting with her, knew she should really. Wasn't that what they had been talking about at church, loving your neighbor? It all sounded so noble and easy to talk about at church. It was a whole other thing to go sit with the new girl with the funny haircut and ugly clothes. What would her other friends say?

   Gideon did the right thing by destroying the idols even though he was afraid and did the destructive deed at night. What do you think Missy should do?

   So Gideon took ten of his servants and did as the LORD told him. But because he was afraid of his family and the townspeople, he did it at night rather than in the daytime. (Judges 6:27)

5. **Question Blitz:** What have your friends or classmates done that you felt wasn't right? What does standing up for what's right reveal about you to others? Who is a "standing up for what's right" role model to you?

6. Staying focused on God throughout the day is (always, sometimes, never) easy for me.

READ OUT LOUD

God's people, the Israelites had forgotten about Jehovah God. The Canaanites, the people who lived near them in the Promised Land, worshiped a false god they named Baal. The Israelites followed the ways of the Canaanites by putting up poles in their backyards to honor Baal. They also constructed outdoor barbeque pits to sacrifice to Baal. (Have a student read out loud Judges 6:25-32 for the story—or have group members read it quietly to themselves.)

ASK

Who is your favorite actor or sports star?

DISCUSS, BY THE NUMBERS

1. Ask your group to describe what Gideon might have felt like living in the midst of a community and family who worshiped false gods. Then discuss where most of the people that surround your group members stand. Ask your group to consider the opportunities they have to talk about Jesus with those around them who aren't committed Christians. What might that look like?

2. Christians have idols even though they are not made of wood, stone, or gold as in Old Testament times. Talk about how easy it can be to worship these.

3. *Idolatry*=devotion to fake gods that distract us from knowing and loving Jesus. This is one definition of idolatry. Remember, even Satan is a fake god, an archangel who wanted to be like God. See if your group can come up with their own definition of idolatry.

4. Read Judges 6:27 out loud. Use this true-to-life situation to talk about what Missy should do. Discuss what it might look like for Missy to act under the cover of darkness as Gideon did versus acting during the day. For example, Missy could get the girl's phone number and call her after school when no one will notice (cover of darkness) or she could be bold and sit with her during lunch. Both would be a good thing to do in the name of Jesus.

> *So Gideon took ten of his servants and did as the LORD told him. But because he was afraid of his family and the townspeople, he did it at night rather than in the daytime. (Judges 6:27)*

5. Work through each of the questions with your group. Ask, "Do you learn more from your identified role model by observing them, talking with them, or both?"

6. Start a faith conversation regarding why it can be difficult to stay focused on God/Jesus throughout the day.

THE CLOSE

The Old Testament, again and again, consistently describes one thing God hates most—idolatry or putting someone or something else before him. God created us in order to be our friend. We were hardwired to love and adore God. Yet, sin separated us from God. Once we have a relationship with Christ, Jesus doesn't want us fooled by false gods. He wants us more than anything to experience his love and forgiveness. But the fake gods of our culture get in the way of that relationship. That's why we need to regularly be reminded of our relationship with Christ. We fellowship with other believers. We participate in worship with our congregation. We study the Bible, pray, and serve others together. All these activities keep us from committing idolatry.

Gideon Does His Utmost for God

God expects us to do our best

1. God's Spirit influenced Gideon to serve God's people. Would you be willing to pray that God's Spirit influences you to serve your congregation?

   ☐ Not really   ☐ Maybe   ☐ Sure

2. Gideon did his best to figure out what God wanted him to do. Who do you know who could walk alongside you as you figure out what God desires for your life?

   ☐ There is really no one.
   ☐ I have family members who might.
   ☐ I know some adults in our congregation who could help.
   ☐ I have some friends who would do it.
   ☐ I have some family friends outside our congregation who might.

3. God had clearly pointed out to Gideon what he was to do—rescue Israel from her enemies. Yet, Gideon wanted additional proof. He wanted reassurance! When do you most need to be reassured by God?

   ☐ When God has asked me to do something that scares me
   ☐ When something bad happens to me
   ☐ When I don't get the prayer answer I wanted
   ☐ When God has asked me to do something I don't want to do
   ☐ When other Christians hurt me
   ☐ When I'm sad
   ☐ Other: _____

4. When has God been the most patient with you?

   ☐ When I have had doubts about Jesus   ☐ When I get down on myself
   ☐ When I don't sense God's presence   ☐ When I'm not acting like a follower of Christ
   ☐ When I'm mad at God   ☐ When I get confused about God's existence
   ☐ When I forget about God

5. What do you think? Y (yes) or N (no)

   _____ God doesn't expect much from me.   _____ I think God is disappointed in me.
   _____ God wants the best for me.   _____ I expect too much from God.
   _____ God expects my church to be more than she is right now.

6. "But Mom," Jeff said. "A *C* isn't a bad grade. It's better than a lot of kids in my math class get. I don't get what you are so upset about."

   "If people see you goofing off and getting bad grades and then they find out you are a Christian, what will they think?" said his mom.

   "That Jesus doesn't care what we do?" said Jeff.

   "Exactly," said his mom. "But he does care and he wants you to care, too."

   What do you think of Jeff's opinion? What do you think of his mom's opinion?

READ OUT LOUD

God's people are again doing evil. The consequences are predictable—they are oppressed for seven long years by the Midianites. They ate Israel's food. They stole Israel's cattle. They ruined Israel's land. When the Israelites had had enough misery they begged the Lord for help. God reminded them of his instructions—worship only me rather than the false gods of your enemies. Then God sends help. (Have a student read out loud the story found in Judges 6:33-40—or have group members read it quietly to themselves.)

ASK

What do your parents expect out of you?

DISCUSS, BY THE NUMBERS

1. Read Judges 6:34 out loud. Tell your group members that God's Holy Spirit dwells inside of them if they are Christ-followers. The indwelling Holy Spirit is nudging them to live for Jesus. Talk together about what they think God is nudging them to do. See how willing they are to pray for God to influence them to serve in your congregation.

   Then the Spirit of the LORD came on Gideon, and he blew a trumpet, summoning the Abiezrites to follow him. (Judges 6:34)

2. Talk about how we need to be diligent in asking God what he wishes us to do. God has high expectations for your group members. But if they take God's calling in their lives lightly they may miss the blessings God has for them. Explore who would be best for your young people to talk with as they try to figure out what God wants them to do.

3. Ask, "How often are you like Gideon—you need proof that God wants you to do something?"

4. Ask, "Why is God so patient with his followers?" Like Gideon we don't deserve God's patience, yet God is compassionate and caring. God is patient when we have doubts about Jesus; when we get down on ourselves; when we don't sense God's presence; when we aren't acting like followers of Christ; when we are mad at God; when we get confused about God's existence; when we forget about God. God's patience is an example of his love for us.

5. See commentary in bold after each statement:
   - God doesn't expect much from me. **No. God has high expectations for all his followers. God has called us to a holy calling (see 2 Timothy 1:9).**
   - I think God is disappointed in me. **No. You are God's creation and have been designed to do good works that God has already prepared for you to get done (see Ephesians 2:10).**
   - God wants the best for me. **Yes. Jesus wants you to have a full life that only he can give you.**
   - I expect too much from God. **This depends on what you expect. God is not your heavenly genie where you rub the God bottle and get your three wishes. But if you expect God to live in and through you so that you can live an exciting Christ-following life then the answer is "Yes."**
   - God expects my church to be more than she is right now. **See what your group members think about how your church is living up to the expectations that God has for her.**

6. Use this as an opportunity to talk practically together about doing our best for God, not through our own power but through the Holy Spirit's power. Possible questions: Wasn't Jeff's mom pushing the Christian thing too much on Jeff? Why shouldn't Jeff be allowed to get C grades, especially in math? Do you think God has higher expectations for Jeff's math grade? Do you think it is right for Jeff's mom to force him to be a witness for the Lord?

THE CLOSE

God expects us to do the best we can because that is how God created us. God doesn't want you to be lazy or cruel or vengeful. As a follower of Jesus, God wants you to be self-disciplined, kind, and to love your enemies. As a Christian, don't you want to show the world that followers of Christ can get great grades, be good in sports, and care about those less fortunate? God has high expectations of you because God created you and knows you are capable of more than you think you are.

Gideon Drafts an Army

We can choose heroes of the faith as our examples

1. If the Lord hadn't reduced the numbers in Gideon's army, the Israelites would have boasted of their achievement apart from God. Of what do you usually boast?

- ❑ My intelligence
- ❑ My great hair
- ❑ My stylish clothes
- ❑ My great athletic ability
- ❑ My popularity
- ❑ My phone
- ❑ My looks
- ❑ My grades
- ❑ My boyfriend/girlfriend
- ❑ My money

2. Gideon's 300 men were warriors of faith. They knew God would fight their battles with them. Other than family members, who do you know who's a great faith warrior, willing to fight God's battles with God as Gideon did?

3. Mark these statements **T (true)** or **F (false)**.

_____ Heroes are for losers.

_____ Heroes will let you down so keep your eyes on Jesus.

_____ Celebrities make great heroes.

_____ Not everyone who attends my church is a hero.

_____ There aren't that many heroes anymore.

4. Most of the men (22,000) in Gideon's army, when given the chance, backed out of their responsibilities due to fear. Most people today are just like these men—they look good on Sunday but Monday through Saturday their faith goes into hibernation. On the line scale below, place an X where you see your faith in Christ during the week.

◆○○○○○○○◆○○○○○○○◆○○○○○○○◆○○○○○○○◆○○○○○○○◆

Faith 24/7/365   What faith?

5. Other than Jesus, who is your favorite Bible hero? Why did you choose this person?

6. Gina and her sister may not get along all the time but Gina really looked up to Angela. She is three years older than Gina, really smart in school, pretty, loves her family and loves God. She was definitely a hard act to follow as a little sister but Gina wanted to be just like her when she got older. Of course she would never tell Angela that.

How is Angela a hero? To whom are you a faith hero?

READ OUT LOUD

Gideon didn't want to lead the Israelite army against her enemies. He made excuses and tried to get out of the job. But Gideon finally stepped up to God's challenge and because of his obedience to God is listed in the Bible Hero Hall of Fame (see Hebrews 11:32). (Have a student read out loud about Gideon's heroics in Judges 7:1-8—or have group members read about them quietly to themselves.)

ASK

Who is your favorite superhero?

DISCUSS, BY THE NUMBERS

1. If the Lord hadn't reduced the numbers in Gideon's army, the Israelites would have boasted of their achievement apart from God (see Judges 7:2). Oftentimes we do the same, thinking our achievements come from us. We are to be self-disciplined and work hard but don't think that our achievements are of our own making. Human effort can achieve great things but remember who created our intelligence and endowed us with creativity. It was God. We don't always give God the credit but God is always part of the achievement picture. We can be proud of our efforts as long as God gets the ultimate glory.

2. Christ-followers don't fight against a physical enemy but against the very powers of darkness. Read Ephesians 6:12 found below. While Gideon did fight against a physical army, his enemies were influenced by the forces of darkness who promoted the false gods whom they worshiped. Lead a faith conversation regarding the reality of evil and God's call to fight that evil. God has called us to transform the world in Jesus' name—to feed the hungry, house the homeless, heal the sick, and share the Good News of Christ's love and forgiveness. Ask, "What can we learn from the names your group members identified about fighting spiritual battles with God?"

> *For our struggle is not against flesh and blood,*
> *but against the rulers, against the authorities,*
> *against the powers of this dark world and*
> *against the spiritual forces of evil in the heav-*
> *enly realms. (Ephesians 6:12)*

3. See commentary in bold after each statement:
   - Heroes are for losers. **False. We all need people we can look to for examples of encouragement, and inspiration.**
   - Heroes will let you down so keep your eyes on Jesus. **Even when heroes disappoint, we still need heroes who can act as examples for us.**
   - Celebrities make great heroes. **False. Most celebrities are anti-heroes.**
   - Not everyone who attends my church is a hero. **Our congregations are filled with hypocrites because we are all sinners.**
   - There aren't that many heroes anymore. **Use this statement to identify today's heroes who are worth emulating.**

4. Lead a faith conversation on how fear gets in the way of your faith. Tell stories of how your faith has been inhibited by fear and how you overcame or are trying to overcome this faith-blocking fear.

5. Talk about how these favorite Bible heroes have inspired your group members to live for Christ.

6. Use this situation to identify the older faith heroes in your congregation. Ask, "Why are they faith heroes?" Talk about how your group members can be faith heroes to the younger members of your congregation.

THE CLOSE

All of us need faith heroes that can be examples of how to live for Jesus. Gideon, though flawed, is one of many faith heroes from the Bible. We also have faith heroes in our congregation that we can look to for inspiration, courage, and examples.

God Helps Gideon Triumph

God overcomes our obstacles every day

1. Gideon has needed repeated reassurances that God was going to give him victory. Do you have problems believing God's promises?

   ☐ All of the time   ☐ Most of the time
   ☐ Some of the time   ☐ None of the time

2. Circle the words that describe facing life's challenges by faith as Gideon tried to do.

   Peaceful   Anxious   Dangerous   Overwhelming   Intense
   Confident   Joyous   Exciting   Boring
   Annoying   Daring   Empowering   Entertaining

3. God promised Gideon a victory. What do you need Jesus to give you a victory over?

   ☐ Getting along with my family
   ☐ Giving in to the wrong things my friends want me to do with them
   ☐ Making fun of others
   ☐ Avoiding my homework
   ☐ My sadness
   ☐ Not wanting to pray or read the Bible
   ☐ Not listening in class
   ☐ My laziness
   ☐ Spreading rumors
   ☐ Doing what is easy
   ☐ My loneliness
   ☐ Feeling bad about myself

4. Gideon's 300-man victory over the 30,000-man Midianite army was God doing the impossible. Would you like to accomplish the impossible with God?

   ☐ For sure   ☐ Maybe   ☐ Not really

5. My faith is stronger than Gideon's faith.

   ☐ Yes   ☐ No   ☐ Not sure

6. Wes hated it when his parents fought. He could be having the best day ever at school and then come home and have it ruined that night by listening to his parents arguing. It was over such stupid stuff, too. Couldn't they see how bad it was for their family?

   How could Wes' faith in Christ help in this situation?

READ OUT LOUD

Always in need of reassurance from God, Gideon is told by God to sneak into the enemy camp. There Gideon hears a Midianite soldier tell of a dream he had that predicted victory for Gideon. Encouraged by what he heard in the Midianite camp, Gideon orders his men to attack using an ingenious strategy. (Have a student read out loud the story from Judges 7:9-22—or have group members read it quietly to themselves.)

ASK

For what have you received a trophy, ribbon, or other award?

DISCUSS, BY THE NUMBERS

1. Ask, "Why do you think, like Gideon, we let our fears stand in the way of us believing God's promises?" Oftentimes, we can't grasp the promise that Jesus will be with us always or that we can give our worries over to God. When we let our fears get the best of us our faith is weakened. Fortunately, like Gideon, God is there to reassure us through prayer, Bible reading, friends, family, sermons, small groups, and our congregation that God's promises are real.

2. Listen to the words your group members circled that describe facing life's challenges by faith as Gideon tried to do. Ask for additional words that they considered. Gideon tried to walk by faith but needed reassurances (walking by sight). Most followers of Christ take three steps forward then two steps back when it comes to faith development. We are all a work in progress. Our faith development is a gradual process that takes a lifetime.

3. Talk about and then pray for the identified victories your group members need in their situations. Your group members can add situations that are not mentioned.

4. God wants to work in us and through us to do the impossible so that we and the world see his glory. As we undertake with God humanly impossible tasks we become more like Jesus. Explore the willingness of your group members to accomplish the impossible with God. Tell a story of how God has worked through you to do great things. Give some examples of difficult tasks that need God working

through us to get them done. Examples: 1) Go on a short-term mission trip; 2) Tell my friends about Jesus; 3) Commit to regularly volunteering at a soup kitchen or other ministry outside our congregation; 4) Start a new ministry; 5) Get my own life on the right track with Jesus; 6) Practice the ways of faith regularly (prayer, Bible reading, worship, faith conversations with others).

5. We grow in our faith as God makes us more like Jesus. It's not a one-shot deal but a lifelong process of faith development. Gideon's faith needed reassurance. Our faith often does as well. Discuss together how your faith and your group members' faith resemble Gideon's faith (needs reassurance; lacks confidence) and unlike Gideon's faith (moves forward without a visible sign of success).

6. Answer the question, "How could Wes' faith in Christ help in this situation?" Christ is present with him. Christ can give him comfort as he suffers through the nightmare of his parents fighting. Christ can be trusted to get Wes through the situation.

THE CLOSE

God was with Gideon even when he doubted or needed reassurance of God working in his life. God gave Gideon the victory. The same can be said today in the lives of followers of Jesus. God gives us victories each and every day. God stands ready to work in our lives to mold and shape us to be more like Jesus. As we submit our will to his will God can accomplish great things through us.

Gideon Turns Away from God

How often do we ditch Jesus?

1. God's people, the Israelites, quickly forgot that God was their ruler. How quickly do you forget about Jesus, Monday through Saturday?

❑ All the time ❑ Sometimes ❑ Rarely/Never

The Israelites said to Gideon, "Rule over us—you, your son and your grandson—because you have saved us from the hand of Midian." (Judges 8:22)

2. God's people didn't feel regret or remorse for wanting to replace God with Gideon as their ruler. They didn't feel sorry for their sins. How often do you feel sorry for your sins?

❑ Every time I sin I feel bad about it.
❑ I sometimes feel bad when I have sinned.
❑ I hardly ever feel bad after I have sinned.

3. Jesus Christ rules over my life—

❑ all of the time ❑ most of the time ❑ some of the time ❑ rarely ❑ never

But Gideon told them, "I will not rule over you, nor will my son rule over you. The LORD will rule over you." (Judges 8:23)

4. Gideon got caught up in the worship of the ephod. I will never be like Gideon and get caught up in worshiping anything other than the Lord.

❑ I strongly agree ❑ I agree ❑ I disagree ❑ I strongly disagree

Gideon made the gold into an ephod, which he placed in Ophrah, his town. All Israel prostituted themselves by worshiping it there, and it became a snare to Gideon and his family. (Judges 8:27)

5. Gideon died and God's people turned back to Baal-worship. When you get out on your own, who or what will you worship?

❑ The God of the Bible ❑ My own accomplishments ❑ I'll pick another religion ❑ Money
❑ I'll probably be an atheist or agnostic ❑ Partying ❑ The divine spark inside of me

No sooner had Gideon died than the Israelites again prostituted themselves to the Baals. They set up Baal-Berith as their god and did not remember the LORD their God, who had rescued them from the hands of all their enemies on every side. (Judges 8:33-34)

6. "Come on, Joey," said Andy, "Come camping with us." It really sounded tempting, but there was only one problem, Andy and his family were going camping on Saturday and not coming back until Sunday afternoon. That meant that Joey would have to miss church. Joey hardly ever missed church, unless he was really sick. It wasn't like his parents made him go, he really liked it. It was just that they probably would think that a camping trip was a good reason to miss worship. So they would be okay with him missing. *Camping really sounded like a lot of fun*, thought Joey. What would it hurt to miss one Sunday—except that he had missed the last two Sundays for soccer?

Do you think Joey is beginning to turn away from Christ?

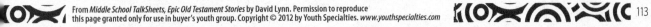

READ OUT LOUD

The battle with the Midianites won, Gideon resists the temptation to be king as the people of Israel request. Gideon knows that only God can be their king. Instead of a kingship, Gideon requested the gold that the soldiers captured. He has an ephod or priestly garment made with the gold. The Israelites, God's people, began to worship the ephod and unfortunately, Gideon and his family were caught up in the idolatry. (Have a student read out loud the story found in Judges 8:22-35—or have group members read it quietly to themselves.)

ASK

When do you feel the most pressure to turn away from God?

DISCUSS, BY THE NUMBERS

1. Read Judges 8:22. Gideon reminded the Israelites that God was to be their King. Discuss together what reminders your group members need to help them remember Jesus.

   The Israelites said to Gideon, "Rule over us—you, your son and your grandson—because you have saved us from the hand of Midian."
   (Judges 8:22)

2. Ask, "How are we like Israel?" "What should we do when we sin?"

3. Read Judges 8:23 out loud. Talk about what it means for Jesus to rule over your life and the lives of your group members. Ask, "Why do you think people want someone or something other than Jesus to rule over their lives?"

4. Read Judges 8:27 out loud. Talk about how Gideon might have gotten caught up in the worship of the ephod. Then explore with your group members how they can avoid the same fate. Look at the importance of continued involvement in your congregation, including regular participation in worship.

   Gideon made the gold into an ephod, which he placed in Ophrah, his town. All Israel prostituted themselves by worshiping it there, and it became a snare to Gideon and his family.
   (Judges 8:27)

5. Read Judges 8:33-34. Even though the Israelites worshiped the ephod, they did not turn to Baal-worship as they had done before Gideon led them (see Judges 6:25). But when Gideon died they quickly turned to Baal-worship. Explore the question, "When you get out on your own, who or what will you worship?" See the commentary in bold after each statement:

- The God of the Bible **Must stay connected to your or another congregation**
- My own accomplishments **Selfishness**
- I'll pick another religion **Islam, Hinduism, Mormonism, Scientology, Jehovah's Witness**
- Money **The love of money (see 1 Timothy 6:10)**
- I'll probably be an atheist or agnostic **Worship science**
- Partying **Hedonism**
- The divine spark inside of me **New Age, influenced by eastern religions such as Hinduism**

   No sooner had Gideon died than the Israelites again prostituted themselves to the Baals. They set up Baal-Berith as their god and did not remember the LORD their God, who had rescued them from the hands of all their enemies on every side. (Judges 8:33-34)

6. Explore why (or why not) Joey is beginning to turn away from Christ. Ask, "What do you think Joey needs to do?" Talk about how like and unlike Joey your group members are.

THE CLOSE

Gideon resisted the temptation to become king upon the insistence of the Israelites. Yet, he and his family got caught up in the worship of the ephod. Before Gideon knew what had happened he had turned from the Lord. We too can get caught up in the world's idols of wealth, happiness, power, and popularity. That's why we stick together as a congregation to encourage each other to grow in our relationship with Christ.

1. Joshua's generation remained faithful to God. Do you think you will remain faithful to the Lord?

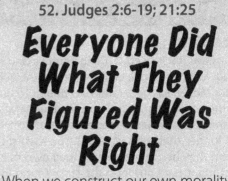

Everyone Did What They Figured Was Right

When we construct our own morality, bad things happen

❑ I will definitely remain faithful to Christ.
❑ I most likely will remain faithful to Jesus.
❑ Maybe I will remain faithful to the Lord.
❑ I know I won't stick with Jesus when I'm older.
❑ I'm not a follower of Christ at this time.

The people served the LORD throughout the lifetime of Joshua and of the elders who outlived him and who had seen all the great things the LORD had done for Israel. (Judges 2:7)

2. Joshua was an incredible leader who encouraged his people to keep following the Lord. Do you encourage your Christian friends to keep following Jesus?

❑ I don't. I'm actually a bad influence on my Christian friends.
❑ I sometimes do.
❑ I often encourage my Christian friends to stick with Jesus.

3. In today's story, the people of Israel were moving away from God. Instead of listening to the Lord they listened only to themselves and what they thought was the right thing to do. How are those at your school or sports team like or unlike the people of Israel?

In those days Israel had no king; everyone did as they saw fit. (Judges 21:25)

4. Check out these statements and decide if you A (agree) or D (disagree).

___ Most of the people my age who I know ignore Jesus Christ.
___ There are consequences for our behaviors.
___ It's okay to do whatever you want as long as you don't hurt someone else.
___ God's opinion matters to me.
___ It's best to follow God's way found in the Bible.

5. Joel couldn't believe his friend Seth. That guy could get away with anything. Joel watched him tell a teacher that he couldn't do his homework because his mom went to the hospital (not true). He also watched him sweet-talk one of the smart girls in class into sharing the answers to the homework that he didn't do. Now as they walked out of a store together Seth showed Joel a package of gum he had taken.
"But that's shoplifting!" said Joel.
"Only if they catch me," said Seth.

What do you think? Are cheating, lying, or stealing okay as long as you don't get caught?

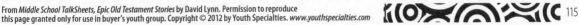

READ OUT LOUD

Israel was not in need of a king because God was their king. Joshua was one of the leaders of the generation after Moses. His generation continued to be faithful to the Lord. But once Joshua and his generation died, many of the people drifted away from God. God was no longer their king. Without God's word to guide them they began to make up their own rules. (Have a student read out loud the story found in Judges 2:6-19; 21:25 to find out what happens when people remove God from their lives—or have group members read about it quietly to themselves.)

ASK

What would happen to you if you came late every day to every class?

DISCUSS, BY THE NUMBERS

1. Ask, "What will you do to remain faithful to Jesus Christ?" Discuss the need for personal prayer and Bible reading along with meeting regularly with other Christians (youth and adults) for worship, prayer, Bible study, fellowship, and faith conversations.
2. Ask, "What kinds of things could you do to motivate your Christian friends to continue to follow Jesus?"
3. Read Judges 21:25 out loud. Ask, "How is the United States today like Israel during the time of the Judges?"
4. See commentary in bold after each statement:
   - Most of the people my age who I know ignore Jesus Christ. **Ask, "What happens when we ignore Jesus Christ?"**
   - There are consequences for our behaviors. **Yes, there are good consequences usually when we make the right decision and bad when we make the wrong decision.**
   - It's okay to do whatever you want as long as you don't hurt someone else. **There are consequences, often bad, when we do whatever we want. God's rules are there to protect us from our own sin and the sin of others.**
   - God's opinion matters to me. **Ask, "Why should God's opinion matter over your opinion or the opinion of your friends or family?"**
   - It's best to follow God's way found in the Bible. **Bad things happen when people make their own moral rules.**
5. This situation is typical of morality today—everything is okay as long as you don't get caught. Talk together about the negative consequences of this moral standard. Discuss why God's opinion matters when we look at right and wrong; whether we get caught or not.

THE CLOSE

Values and ethical standards matter. That's why God gave the Ten Commandments. We need boundaries around our behavior to protect us as individuals and as a society. When people no longer care about God's opinion, they begin to make up their own rules. Decisions about right and wrong become relative. The last verse in the last chapter of Judges describes this kind of ethical decision-making. "In those days Israel had no king; everyone did as they saw fit." (Judges 21:25) Is this how you want to decide right and wrong? Or maybe you care about God's opinion!

High School TalkSheets

50 Ready-to-Use Discussions on the Life of Christ

Terry Linhart

Your high school students probably think they know a lot about Jesus. But do they know how the stories of Jesus' life relate to their own? If you want to get them thinking and talking about Jesus—who he really was, and what that means for them today—you have everything you need right here.

The latest addition to the best-selling TalkSheets series, *High School TalkSheets: Life of Christ* gives you easy-to-use discussion starters and the tools to lead students into meaningful dialogue about Jesus. The one-page, reproducible handouts offer provocative questions in a compelling design that cover everything from the prediction of his birth to his ascension. Students will delve into each aspect of Jesus' life while looking at it through the lens of their own world and applying it to their own lives. These TalkSheets present every aspect of Jesus' life in a way that young teens can connect with as they learn to apply the lessons to their own lives.

TalkSheets makes the Bible relevant and engaging for students, while offering helpful hints and optional activities to help your youth ministry team effectively facilitate great conversations—without a lot of prep work.

Available in stores and online!

Middle School TalkSheets

50 Ready-to-Use Discussions on the Life of Christ

Terry Linhart

It's not hard to get middle schoolers to talk...unless you're talking about something other than the latest band, movie, or the opposite sex! If you want to get them thinking and talking about Jesus—beyond the flannelgraph, Sunday school Jesus—you have everything you need right here.

The latest addition to the best-selling TalkSheets series, *Middle School TalkSheets: Life of Christ* gives you easy-to-use discussion starters and the tools to lead students into meaningful dialogue about Jesus. The one-page, reproducible handouts offer provocative questions in a compelling design that keep in mind the unique challenges of middle school discussions. These TalkSheets present every aspect of Jesus' life in a way that young teens can connect with as they learn to apply the lessons to their own lives.

TalkSheets makes the Bible relevant and engaging for students, while offering helpful hints and optional activities to help your youth ministry team effectively facilitate great conversations—without a lot of prep work.

Available in stores and online!

ZONDERVAN®
.com

High School TalkSheets on the New Testament, Epic Bible Stories

52 Ready-to-Use Discussions

David Lynn

The teenagers in your youth group love to talk about epic things—whether it's the latest blockbuster movie or a new song from their favorite band. Now you can get them talking about the epic stories found in the New Testament.

The best-selling TalkSheets series brings you an epic discussion starter in *High School TalkSheets on the New Testament, Epic Bible Stories: 52 Ready-to-Use Discussions*. The one-page, reproducible handouts are compelling and thought provoking. Not only that, they're easy for you to use: You'll find helpful hints and optional activities that can help facilitate great conversations.

Using the TalkSheets in this book, your high school students will explore and talk about epic stories like:

- Jesus' Birth
- The Teenage Jesus
- Jesus Raises a Widow's Son to Life
- Jesus Walks on Water
- Mary & Martha
- A Shriveled Fig Tree Object Lesson
- Jesus Before Pilate

- The Great Commission
- Peter & John Can't Keep Quiet
- Ananias & Sapphira Are Dead Wrong
- Barnabas, The Encourager
- Paul Before King Agrippa
- And many, many more!

Available in stores and online!

More Middle School TalkSheets on the New Testament, Epic Bible Stories

52 Ready-to-Use Discussionst

David Lynn

Every blockbuster movie with an epic story that you've seen has come back with a sequel. Think of "Star Wars" or "Lord of the Rings." Why should a TalkSheets book be any different? With the epic stories found in the New Testament, we couldn't cover it all in one edition of TalkSheets...so we're back with more!

More Middle School TalkSheets on the New Testament, Epic Bible Stories brings another year's worth of compelling and thought provoking weekly discussion starters to your middle school youth group, leading to meaningful conversations among the students in your group. Not only that, they're easy for you to use: You'll find helpful hints and optional activities that help facilitate great conversations.

With the reproducible TalkSheets in this book, you'll help your middle school students look closer at some of the epic stories of the New Testament, like:

- Jesus eats dinner with a bunch of sinners
- Peter demonstrates evangelism
- Jesus preaches for six hours
- Peter makes a jail break
- Jesus tells a story of the rich man and Lazarus
- And many more!

Available in stores and online!

ZONDERVAN®
.com

Share Your Thoughts

With the Author: Your comments will be forwarded to the author when you send them to *zauthor@zondervan.com*.

With Zondervan: Submit your review of this book by writing to *zreview@zondervan.com*.

Free Online Resources at

www.zondervan.com

Zondervan AuthorTracker: Be notified whenever your favorite authors publish new books, go on tour, or post an update about what's happening in their lives at www.zondervan.com/authortracker.

Daily Bible Verses and Devotions: Enrich your life with daily Bible verses or devotions that help you start every morning focused on God. Visit www.zondervan.com/newsletters.

Free Email Publications: Sign up for newsletters on Christian living, academic resources, church ministry, fiction, children's resources, and more. Visit www.zondervan.com/newsletters.

Zondervan Bible Search: Find and compare Bible passages in a variety of translations at www.biblegateway.com.

Other Benefits: Register yourself to receive online benefits like coupons and special offers, or to participate in research.